EDITING TODAY WORKBOOK

SECOND EDITION

EDITING
TODAY
WORKBOOK

SECOND EDITION

RON F. SMITH

 **Iowa State Press**
A Blackwell Publishing Company

Ron F. Smith is a professor of journalism at the University of Central Florida in Orlando. He has worked for newspapers in Indiana, Ohio and Florida, and is an active member of the Society of Professional Journalists and serves on the board of the Central Florida chapter. Smith has published numerous articles in *Journalism Quarterly, Newspaper Research Journal, Collegiate Journalist, Quill* and *Journalism Educator.* He co-authored *Groping for Ethics in Journalism* with Gene Goodwin and assumed sole authorship on the fourth edition.

©2003 Iowa State Press
A Blackwell Publishing Company
All rights reserved

Iowa State Press
2121 State Avenue, Ames, Iowa 50014

Orders: 1-800-862-6657
Office: 1-515-292-0140
Fax: 1-515-292-3348
Web site: www.iowastatepress.com

♾ Printed on acid-free paper in the United States of America

First edition, © 1996, Iowa State University Press
Second edition, ©2003, Iowa State Press

International Standard Book Number: 0-8138-1317-4

CONTENTS

INTRODUCTION

WHY STUDY EDITING?

You may already be thinking about life after college. You're pretty sure that you want a career that involves working in print media: newspapers, magazines, newsletters, online news services. But you're not sure in what capacity.

Consider editing.

Despite what you may have heard about the job market for journalists, there's a shortage of copy editors. Newspapers have trouble filling openings on their copy desks. Although large newspapers get hundreds of applications for every reporting position, they often have to advertise in *Editor & Publisher* to find copy editors.

However, the possibility of finding a job shouldn't be your only motivation for considering an editing career.

Editing has many pluses. Editors have the satisfaction of knowing that their work contributes directly to the quality of the publication.

Assignment editors know they are the ones who find inaccuracies in the reporter's first draft, suggest additional sources for the reporter to check and help shape the story into something readable. And copy editors know they are the last editorial employees to see a story before it goes into print. When they catch errors, they save the reporter and the publication some embarrassment. They also get to display creativity in the headlines they write and the pages they design. A well-worded headline can mean the difference between a story that is read and one that readers skip, and design can help attract readers to stories they might otherwise overlook.

Many people prefer life on the desk to life on the streets as reporters. There's often more camaraderie among copy editors than among reporters. And they don't have to put up with many of the frustrations that reporters encounter: Copy editors never face the anxiety of tracking down a source on deadline or of wrangling with people reluctant to part with information.

WHAT DOES IT TAKE TO BE A COPY EDITOR?

Skills beginning copy editors need	Skills new j-grads lack
1. Grammar, spelling and punctuation.	1. Grammar, spelling and punctuation.
2. Accuracy and fact-checking.	2. Editing wordiness, clarity and sentence structure.
3. Editing wordiness, clarity and sentence structure.	3. Headline writing.
4. General knowledge.	4. Accuracy and fact-checking.
5. Story structure, organization and content.	5. General knowledge.
6. Ethical concerns.	6. Associated Press style and usage.
7. Headline writing.	7. Story structure, organization and content.
8. Analytical/critical thinking.	8. Understanding numbers.
9. Associated Press style and usage.	9. Layout and page design.
10. Cutline writing.	10. News judgment and story selection.

Why is there a glut of applications for reporting positions and a shortage of copy editors? Three reasons come to mind. The first is obvious. Many people prefer reporting: They like tracking down stories and meeting people. The second reason is a lack of awareness of deskwork. Many people don't know what copy editors do and therefore never consider becoming one. The third reason is that many journalism graduates just don't have the skills necessary to get and keep an editing job.

What skills do you need to be a copy editor? Journalism Professor Ann Auman asked newspaper editors to list the skills that they expected newly hired copy editors to have. They told her the most important skill was the ability to correct grammar, spelling and punctuation. Second on their list was the ability to check for accuracy and factual errors. Third was the ability to recognize and remedy wordy, poorly written stories.

They placed much less importance in computer skills. At No. 13 was "mechanics of computer editing," No. 21 was "software for layout/pagination," and tied at 25 (the bottom of the list) were "software for graphics" and "computer photo editing." Then Auman asked the editors to judge the abilities of the journalism graduates they had hired recently. Most said they weren't too happy with them. The No. 1 trouble spot? Grammar, spelling and punctuation.[1]

Grammar, spelling, punctuation? You may be surprised, but your editing instructor may not be. For years, editors have complained to journalism schools that too many journalism graduates lack basic English skills. Editors have become so doubtful of journalism graduates' abilities that most newspapers now require grammar, punctuation, style and spelling tests to weed out inadequately prepared applicants.

IS GOOD GRAMMAR ALL YOU NEED?

Of course, there's more to editing than fixing grammar and punctuation. Among the attributes of successful copy editors are good news judgment, a quick wit, analytical skills, knowledge of typography and graphics, an understanding of their communities, a background in history and politics, and a familiarity with basic math and statistics. You will develop some of those attributes in your journalism courses and in general education courses and electives. But, much of what you'll need you must learn on your own, by reading widely, listening to people and participating in your community.

In this workbook, we start with the basics of grammar, punctuation and word usage. No, this isn't the fun or creative part of editing. However, many professions require a set of basic knowledge before the practitioners can become creative. Architects must learn how much weight a steel beam can support before they begin to design skyscrapers. Surgeons must learn to use scalpels before they attempt heart transplants. Copy editors must clean up all the grammar and punctuation problems in a story before they begin working on its lead and revising sentences. After a refresher course in grammar and Associated Press style, you'll be asked to watch for wordiness, bad writing, inadequate reporting, libel and unfairness.

At first you may discover that you miss many errors in the exercises because you read over them. However, with practice, you will learn a new way of reading: a slow, deliberate way. Soon, you'll be challenging every comma, every reference, and every name. The copy you have edited will be free of errors.

ON DEVELOPING RED LIGHTS AND MEMORIZING THE AP STYLEBOOK

No one expects you to memorize the stylebook or a grammar text. Few copy editors know every detail in the *AP Stylebook*. Instead, they've developed a series of "red lights" that alert them to potential problems.

You already have some red lights. When you write sentences with "who" or "whom" or with "lie" or "lay," you probably pause and try to figure out which word is correct. In effect, a warning has gone off in your brain cautioning you to be careful.

As you go through this book, you'll develop more of these red lights. For example, you will become aware of words that can be used improperly. Then you will check the stylebook and make any needed corrections.

Editing on this level takes diligence and discipline. You will be expected to question every detail in a story and to look up the things you don't know. This will seem awkward at first. But soon, you will notice three changes in your performance. First, you'll soon find yourself finding errors you would have read over before. Second, you'll begin to find information in stylebooks and dictionaries more easily. Third, you'll begin to find mistakes in your own writing before you give your stories to your instructors or editors.

THE NEW EDITION

This new edition of the workbook maintains the emphasis on the basic skills: grammar, punctuation and word usage. We've made two changes. You may have noticed that one complaint editors had about journalism graduates is that they don't understand numbers. You may not like math, but you will have to admit that a lot of stories have numbers. Taxes are going up 5 percent, crime is 10 percent lower this year, the median home costs $120,000, girls score 10 percent higher on the admissions tests, and on and on. To help you feel more comfortable with numbers, we've added a math section and included more math concerns in the stories.

The second change is that we have added lots of new stories. We hope these stories are more like those you might encounter if you begin your career at a decent daily.

USING THIS WORKBOOK

If your school offers only a one-semester editing class, your instructor will have trouble covering all the material. Fifteen weeks isn't very long to cover grammar, punctuation, content editing, headline writing, graphics, typography and page design. Unfortunately, your instructor may have to pass over some topics rather quickly. That places more of the burden of preparing for a journalism career on your shoulders.

We've designed this workbook so that you can do many exercises on your own. The answers to the first set of exercises in every section are at the back of the book. If your instructor does not have time to go through the crash course in grammar, we would suggest you do the exercises and check your answers. If you do well on them, then you can go on to the next section. However, if your answers don't jibe with the ones in the back of the book, you might want to review that section.

Remember that even if your instructors do not spend time discussing basic grammar, they will still expect you to correct grammar errors in the stories you edit and to make sure your own stories are grammatically correct.

Finally, *don't believe anything you read in these exercises.* The Northern State University in this workbook does not refer to any real university, and none of the people mentioned really exists. Some exercises have been inspired by events that were reported in papers where I've worked or in papers that I read regularly, including *Orlando Sentinel, Tampa Tribune* and *South Florida Sun-Sentinel.* Yet, the "facts" in these exercises bear no relationship to the real world.

Ron F. Smith
University of Central Florida
Orlando, FL 32816
rsmith@pegasus.cc.ucf.edu

NOTES

1. Ann Auman, "A Lesson for Instructors: Top 10 Copy-Editing Skills," *Journalism and Mass Communication Educator,* Autumn 1995, 12–20.

EDITING TODAY WORKBOOK

SECOND EDITION

CHAPTERS **1** AND **2**

THE COPY EDITOR'S JOB

SECTION 1: COACHING AND EDITING STORIES

Reporters work directly with their editors. We've given these editors the generic titles "assignment editor" and "line editor." In most newsrooms, they have specific titles such as assistant metro editor, city editor, features editor or bureau chief. These editors assign stories or approve reporters' ideas for stories, and they do the first-read editing of them.

First-read or content editing means checking the organization, clarity and tone of the story and making sure the proper sources have been contacted so that the story is fair and complete. First-read editors also clean up any writing and grammar problems they find. Because so much of their editing concerns the content of the stories, some people call it "content editing."

Many assignment editors see themselves as coaches. They discuss story ideas with their reporters, make suggestions as they are gathering the information, and then confer with reporters as they are editing their stories. They try not to rewrite the stories themselves but rather to give guidance to reporters on how they can improve their own stories.

After assignment editors have finished editing the story, it is sent to the copy desk. Among the responsibilities of copy editors are

- Rechecking the clarity, organization, fairness and completeness of the story. If they have questions, they may discuss the story with the copy-desk chief, the assignment editor or sometimes the reporter.
- Making sure that the story is accurate.
- Cleaning up the grammar, style, spelling, punctuation, word usage and other writing problems in the story.
- Writing the headline.
- At many papers, designing pages.

No copy editor ever knows enough. But copy editors have a suspicious streak that drives them to check reference materials, the Internet and the *AP Stylebook*. They don't guess at facts.

Copy editors are the last people to see the story. Any errors they leave in a story will appear in the publication. For that reason, copy editors must be very exacting people who have the discipline needed to check every detail and correct the errors they find.

EXERCISE 1   NAME _____

Answer these questions from your reading of Chapter 1.

1. In Chapter 1 of *Editing Today*, we looked at the relationship between reporter Michelle Bearden and her assignment editor Penny Carnathan. Find three specific places where Carnathan improved the story.

2. Many writers call relationships like the one between Carnathan and Bearden "coaching." What do they mean by coaching and how did Carnathan coach Bearden?

3. After Carnathan finished editing the story, she sent it to the copy desk. Compare the duties of the copy editor to those of an assignment editor such as Carnathan.

4. Practice coaching. Give a story you've written in a writing class or for the campus paper to another student in class. Ask the person to "coach" your story, that is, to point out things you've done well and to suggest areas for improvement. Then trade roles. You coach the other student using a story that the student has written. After you've been both reporter and coach, answer these questions:

   a. How did it feel as you were being coached? What did you learn about your reporting and your writing?

   b. How did it feel being a coach? Did you find that you could find areas for improvement in the other student's work more readily than you can find them in your own?

   c. How do you think you would have felt if you had been the reporter and the editor had simply rewritten the story? How would you have felt if you were the editor and had been called upon to rewrite the story?

   d. What conclusions can you make about the importance of coaching?

5. At many papers, reporters and editors discuss story possibilities. One approach is called *mapping*. It works like this: Reporters and editors take an ordinary event such as a traffic accident involving a cyclist. Then they ask questions that might move the story beyond the mundane. The idea is not to ask questions such as "What was the name of the cyclist?" Instead, they may wonder "How dangerous is that intersection?" or "How many students are hurt riding to school?" or "Why aren't there more bike lanes?" Often they discover many ideas for good stories.

   a. Take an ordinary event you've seen on campus or in your community. Come up with at least 15 possible story ideas.

   b. Go through your 15 ideas and pick the three that you think might make the best stories.

6. *The Tampa Tribune* is one of the leaders in convergence. The text described how Bearden covered a story. In addition to the regular newspaper reporting, what kinds of things did Bearden do to prepare the story for other media?

7. Think about your own career. What advantages would there be to work at a converged newspaper? What disadvantages might there be?

8. Kiely Agliano, who designed the page with Bearden's story, says she thinks of herself as a journalist, not an artist. What distinction is she making?

9. Many news Web sites would rather hire journalism graduates than computer-science majors. From your reading of the operations of TBO.com, can you think of reasons for this?

EXERCISE 2   NAME _____

Answer these questions from your reading of Chapter 1.

1. What are some of the advantages of working on the desk?
2. What are some of the disadvantages of working on the desk?
3. What are the differences between universal desks and specialized desks?
4. What is meant by these phrases?
   a. copy flow
   b. budget meeting
   c. zoned editions
5. What is the "maestro" system? How might this system help (a) reporters? (b) page designers? (c) photographers? (d) graphic journalists (artists)?
6. *Pagination* is a term used for the production of pages with computers. What advantages might pagination have for editors? What disadvantages?
7. Many students try to edit papers as carefully as they can before giving them to their professors. Then, when they get the papers back, they are surprised at the "silly" mistakes they made. From your reading of the textbook, why didn't they catch the errors before they turned them in?
8. The text suggests that good editors read slowly. Why would reading slowly be an advantage to copy editors?

EXERCISE 3   NAME _____

You can answer most of the following questions using standard reference books, the Internet, and computer databases available in your library. Answer them and list the source you used.

1. A feature story quotes an actor as saying his favorite novels are *Racer's Edge* by Somerset Maugham and *The Prophet* by Kahlil Gibran. You want to check to make sure those titles and names are right. What are the correct titles and how do you spell the names of the authors?

2. A story quotes several doctors whose medical degrees were obtained from the following: (a) Hopkins, (b) UCLA, (c) Southern Cal, (d) Ole Miss, (e) Berkeley. You want to give the full names of the schools. What are they? In what cities are these schools?

3. A reporter known for overstating his facts writes a story about what he calls "the half-million-dollar traffic accident." He claims that is the cost of the two cars involved. One was a Lamborgini; the other an Austin Martin. Calling it a half-million-dollar wreck is fun, but you want to make sure it's not an exaggeration. Could those two cars be that expensive? And what about the spelling of the car names?

4. You're editing a story about the media's reluctance to deal with complaints. You recall from an ethics seminar that Minnesota had some sort of press council that heard the public's concerns. Is it still in business? If so, you want to show a recent case. Describe one. What's your source?

5. What are the correct names of the daily newspapers in Fort Worth? Portland, Ore.? Portland, Maine? New Orleans? St. Louis? (Remember that some papers use *The* as part of their names; also, some names have hyphens.)

6. A defendant in a murder trial is described as having an IQ of 65. That sounds low. What would be an accurate way to describe his IQ so that readers can understand what it means to have an IQ of 65?

7. A Boeing 737 has crashed near the local airport. An editor asks you to find out as much as you can about that type of aircraft. When were the first ones built? How many engines do they have?

8. A county judge is arrested for drunken driving. In her purse, police find two bottles of lorazepam. What is that drug? What's it used for?

9. The dean of students at a local university is the state's youngest university administrator. For spring break, she goes to Daytona Beach with a group of students. She gets a little too much into the spirit of things and is arrested for indecent exposure. You aren't sure how serious that charge is in Florida. It's close to deadline and you know Florida has good public records laws with Internet access. In Florida, is indecent exposure a felony or a misdemeanor? What could the dean's sentence be if she is convicted?

10. Does Washington, D.C., have representation in Congress? Does Puerto Rico? If so, name the current representatives and/or senators.

11. A columnist accuses the president of the student government of telling the biggest lie since Richard Nixon said, "I'm not a crook." Not only are you worried about the prospect of libeling the student, you suspect that the reporter got the quote wrong. What did Nixon say?

12. In a travel story, the writer suggests that you tip bellhops two pounds in London and five euros in Paris. You want to give readers an estimation of how much those tips are in U.S. currency. What are they worth?

EXERCISE 4   NAME _____

You can answer most of the following questions using standard reference books, the Internet, and computer databases available in your library. Answer them and list the source you used.

1. The president of a local community college has died—right on your deadline. The reporter has confirmed that the death was due to complications after surgery. The surgery was a gastric bypass. You don't want to use the medical term without any explanation, but the reporter wasn't able to ask hospital sources. What is a gastric bypass?

2. You're editing a feature about a local professor. He has written a book that he says is about "economic turmoil in my native Bangladesh." But when describing the professor's background, the reporter wrote that the professor was born in Pakistan. How can someone be a native of both Bangladesh and Pakistan? How could you clear that up for readers?

3. Objecting to a plea agreement offered by a prosecutor, a lawyer said her client was faced with a "Hobson's choice." What does she mean?

4. In a column, your rock critic wrote that VH1 named "(I Can't Get No) Satisfaction" by the Rolling Stones the best rock song ever. She says the song was written in Clearwater, Fla. But she didn't give the year or the name of the album on which the song first appeared. (Vinyl "albums" were primitive forerunners of the CD.) What year and on what album did the song *first* appear? (It was on several Stones' albums.) She spelled it Rolling Stones, but you think your roommate has a CD that says Rollin' Stones. Which is correct?

5. After his plans were leaked to the media, a senator said the leak "proves Abe Lincoln was right: Two can keep a secret only if one of them is dead." The quotation doesn't sound right to you, and it doesn't sound at all like Lincoln. Who said it and what is the correct quotation?

6. You need some information about a man who is serving time in a state prison. You know that in many states, this information is available online. What's the Internet address (the URL) of the site, if there is one, in your state? Are county property records online where you live? If so, what's the address?

7. A reporter compares the possible TV coverage of a local murder trial with the one involving former football player O.J. Simpson. The reporter wrote that that trial was in the early 1990s in California. You want to be a little more specific. What year was the trial and where did it take place?

8. A columnist is making fun of efforts to crack down on drinking at university football games. She says that Americans have been allowed to drink since the 19th Amendment was passed 50 years ago. You don't trust her history. Is she right?

9. A reporter has written a feature about powerful women in government. You think he has misspelled some names. What are the correct spellings of the names of the women justices on the Supreme Court?

10. In a travel story, the writer mentions Dinosaur National Park but doesn't tell where it is. Is the name right? What might be a good way of describing where it is?

11. How many votes did the Democratic candidate for president in the last election get in the county where you live? How many did the Republican get?

12. Name a newspaper owned by the following companies: the Tribune Company (other than the *Chicago Tribune*); Knight-Ridder; the *New York Times* (other than the *Times*); Gannett (other than *USA Today*); and the Belo Company.

SECTION 2: CHECKING FACTS IN THE *AP STYLEBOOK*

You've already been introduced to the AP Stylebook in your first newswriting class. Your instructors expected you to abide by its rules as you wrote your stories. But the stylebook is of even greater importance to copy editors. They rely on it for guidance on at least five kinds of issues:

1. The stylebook lists the rules explaining when to abbreviate and capitalize words and when to use figures. Clearly, these rules are arbitrary: They were created by committees of editors. But they are the law at most papers.
2. The stylebook mandates preferred spellings. Lots of words have more than one spelling: *adviser* or *advisor, ax* or *axe, canceled* or *cancelled*, and *goodbye, goodby* or *good-bye*. You'll find each of these spellings in dictionaries. But newspapers want to be consistent. The stylebook tells which spelling to use. It also gives preferred spellings for many corporate, governmental and political entities.
3. The stylebook explains many grammatical problems. Copy editors often run into grammatical constructions they aren't sure are right. The stylebook may have the answer.
4. The stylebook explains word usage. Copy editors do not want to let the wrong word slip into the paper. They guard against mix-ups in words such as *concrete* and *cement, continual* and *continuous, adverse* and *averse, between* and *among, convince* and *persuade*, and *arbitration* and *mediation*. The stylebook is a good place to check the words you aren't sure of.
5. The stylebook also has lots of information that editors use to check the accuracy of stories and to gain background. You'll find facts about business, weather, sports, firearms, names of organizations, governmental bodies, religion and other topics. (As with any reference book, the information in the stylebook becomes outdated. If the facts in the story are different from information in the stylebook, you should question the reporter. But don't change copy unless you're sure you're right.)

Besides the AP Stylebook, many newspapers also have their own supplementary stylebooks as well as their preferred dictionary, which often serve these functions:

1. They may give guidance on sensitive questions. They may specify the paper's preferences for calling people *gay* or *homosexual*, using *black* or *African-American* or describing pickets at an abortion clinic as *pro-life* or *anti-abortion*.
2. They may give style rules for and explain the functions of local governmental and police agencies. Laws and procedures vary from jurisdiction to jurisdiction. Stylebooks often explain some of these peculiarities and spell out how the paper handles them. An example: In some states, counties have both county commissions and county councils. Stylebooks may explain each body's responsibilities.
3. They give correct spellings and rules for abbreviations on second reference for local businesses and the names of groups, streets, buildings, airports, and so on. Stylebooks in Florida remind reporters and editors that a major north-south toll road is "Florida's Turnpike," not "The Florida Turnpike." The *Atlanta Journal-Constitution*'s style supplement clears up some myths about the death of Margaret Mitchell, the author of *Gone With the Wind*. When the Olympics were held in Atlanta in 1996, the *Journal-Constitution* added a section with guidelines for stories about the Games.
4. Some include the newspaper's ethics code and synopses of state and local laws affecting the media. These ethics codes often explain the paper's rules on accepting free tickets and gifts, writing free-lance articles, and avoiding financial and social conflicts of interests. Many include guidelines for naming rape victims, identifying juvenile offenders and dealing with belligerent readers.

Unfortunately, the AP Stylebook doesn't make a lot of its information easy to find. For example, in many editions of the *AP Stylebook*, if you want to know whether *shape-up* is hyphenated, you can find the answer by looking up *shape-up* in the S section of the main part of the *Stylebook*. But if you want to know whether *makeup* is hyphenated, you have to turn to the U section and check under *-up*.

Finding information is made even more challenging because most editions of the stylebook have sections near the back that discuss business, sports, computer terminology, punctuation and media law. Occasionally, you'll find some information about a topic has been placed in the main section of the book but other bits of information about the same topic are in these special sections.

The lesson to be learned? It's a good idea to become familiar with the stylebook now. After you begin to figure out its organization, you'll find information more quickly. The time you spend looking through the stylebook now will save you time when you're taking a test in your editing class in a few weeks—or trying to meet a deadline in a newsroom in a couple of months. Following are exercises that introduce the variety of information that's in the *AP Stylebook*.

EXERCISE 5   NAME _____

Use the *AP Stylebook* to answer these questions. You will need no other reference.

1. A soccer team from an area high school is playing in a tourney in July in England. A story from an English reporter makes a big deal about the temperature. It's 35 degrees. You know that's Celsius. What would it be in Fahrenheit?

2. An obituary says the deceased attended "Church of Christ, Scientist." Is that name correct?

3. Scientists have changed their minds. The earthquake in Oregon yesterday was 5.5 on the Richter scale, not 4.5. How much more severe do they now think the quake was? In everyday language, how much damage would you expect?

4. It's a bad time for pizzerias. A story says one pizza place filed for Chapter 11 bankruptcy while another filed for Chapter 7 bankruptcy. What's the difference?

5. A business story talks about Fannie Mae and Freddie Mac. Who or what are they? Are those the right names?

6. A story sometimes uses the terms *monetary* and *fiscal* when referring to the same things. What do these words mean?

7. You're editing a front-page story about the efforts of your community to get a minor-league hockey team. The story says that during recent negotiations, the mayor scored a "hat trick" when the team agreed to move to your city, pay rent for the city-owned arena and supervise a youth hockey league. You've never seen the mayor wear a hat or do tricks. What does that phrase mean? What point was the writer making by using that term?

8. A story quotes a financial adviser who recommends that people buy stocks but not bonds in European corporations. What's the difference between stocks and bonds?

9. A free-lancer does a travel story about Quebec. She writes about how friendly the Canucks were. Who are they? Is the term OK?

10. One story refers to a clergyman at a local Baptist church as a minister, whereas another story calls a clergyman at the same church a pastor. Which is right?

11. A story says that two ships were traveling at 20 knots per hour when they crashed. How fast were they going in miles per hour? Is the phrase "knots per hour" correct?

12. You're editing a story that has this sentence: "Canada is a member of the British Commonwealth." You thought that Canada was an independent nation. Does the writer have his facts right?

13. A typhoon hit the east coast of Japan on the same day that a hurricane slammed into Puerto Rico. You're considering combining these stories into a package about disasters, but you don't want to force a comparison of dissimilar events. How do typhoons differ from hurricanes? Do you think it would be acceptable to put stories about them in one package?

14. In some parts of a story, the reporter called a religious organization "evangelical," and at other places she called it "fundamentalist." She seems to use these terms interchangeably. Is that proper? What concerns should you have when using those words?

15. Is Notre Dame in the Big 10? Is it Big 10, Big-10 or Big Ten? Is San Diego State in the Pac 10? Is it Pac 10, Pac-10 or Pac Ten?

16. A news report says that most of the Midwest is having heavy snows and that portions of Michigan are being hit by blizzards. Aren't heavy snows and blizzards the same thing? If not, what are the differences?

17. What are the differences between a movie that the Motion Picture Association of America gives an X rating and one that it gives an NC-17 rating?

18. Spell and capitalize these words as the AP does: teleprompter, the du pont family, realtor, popsicle, french fries, dumpster, frisbee, dow jones co., swiss cheese, basset hound, boston beans, kmart, dr pepper, jello.

19. You're editing a story reporting that the police chief wanted his officers to have more firepower. According to the story, he replaced their .38-caliber revolvers with .45-caliber semiautomatics and their 20-gauge shotguns with 12-gauge shotguns. What's the difference between a .38-caliber weapon and a .45-caliber one? What's the difference between a revolver and a semiautomatic? And if the chief wants more firepower, why did he select smaller shotguns?

20. Spell, hyphenate and capitalize these computer-oriented words as the *AP Stylebook* does: email, web, internet, ram, cd, word processing.

SECTION 3: THE BASICS OF AP STYLE

A story reports that one contractor bid $1,600,000 to build a school whereas another bid $1.6 million. How many readers would be confused by the inconsistency in the way the numbers are written? A few might be, but most could probably figure out what was meant. And, if one story referred to "Representative Charles Long" and then called him "Mr. Long" on subsequent reference while another story called him "Rep. Charles Long" and shortened his name to "Long" from then on, your readers would still understand the stories. But they will notice these inconsistencies, and they may consider your newspaper less professional because of them.

To head off these discrepancies, newspapers have stylebooks, which are filled with arbitrary decisions made primarily to ensure consistency. An important word in that description is *arbitrary*. There's no sensible explanation for why *senator* should be abbreviated before names (Sen. John Doe) but *president* should be spelled out (President Jane Doe). But it's the rule, and reporters and editors are expected to abide by it.

In this workbook, we concentrate on the style decisions of the Associated Press. That's because throughout your newspaper career, you'll probably be using AP style. Although a few large newspapers such as the *New York Times* and *Washington Post* have their own stylebooks, most American papers use the *AP Stylebook* and supplement it with lists of local rules and exceptions. So now is a good time to become familiar with it.

Numbers nine and below are usually written as words. For numbers 10 and above, figures are usually used. Numbers of a million or more take this form: 1 million, 4.5 million, $23 million, $1.6 billion. Those rules hold true with numbers in a series:

The jury has 10 women and two men.
Officials estimate that 12 million to 15 million people may have the disease. (Not 12 to 15 million, to avoid confusing readers about the size of the spread)

The rules also apply to ordinal numbers:

The accident blocked traffic on 11th Street and Fifth Avenue.
The first time was difficult, but by the 10th try everyone was doing well.
The seventh graders were too small to play the 10th graders.
He closed his restaurant on 11th Avenue and opened a new one on Second Street.

Exceptions abound when dealing with numbers. We discuss two common ones.

Exception 1: Scores, vote totals, dimensions, dates, times, percentages, money amounts and ages are always figures. Decades are followed by an *s* with no apostrophe before the *s*, as in *'70s* and *'80s*. (An apostrophe is used before the figure to indicate that part of the number has been omitted.)

The jury deadlocked 9–3 for conviction.
The 7-footer had trouble fitting into the 2-foot-wide seat.
The baby weighed 5 pounds, 8 ounces.
Voting begins at 7:30 a.m. and ends at 7 p.m. July 2.
Only 7 percent of NSU students favor the plan.
A 3-year-old girl bought the $8 ticket for 5 cents.
She was in her 20s in the '90s.
A record low in Tallahassee, Fla., is 5 degrees.

Exception 2: Short numbers at the beginning of sentences are spelled out. Sentences that begin with longer numbers are usually recast:

Not: 12 men were charged with gambling.
But: Twelve men were charged with gambling.
Or: Police charged 12 men with gambling.

Not: One hundred forty-three fans were escorted from the stadium after the incident.
But: After the incident, 143 fans were escorted from the stadium.
Or: Officials escorted 143 fans from the stadium after the incident.

Street, avenue, and **boulevard** are abbreviated when addresses have street numbers; they are spelled out when the numbers aren't present. Directions such as *north*, *south*, *east* and *west* follow the same pattern. Other words used in addresses such as *circle, drive, trail, trace* and so on are always spelled out.

He moved to 234 S. Fifth St. from South Butler Drive.
He moved to South Fifth Street from 562 S. Butler Drive.

She bought a house at 1534 W. 14th Ave.
She bought a house on West 14th Avenue.

State names are abbreviated when they come after city names; otherwise, they are spelled out. Newspapers have been slow to adopt the two-letter postal abbreviations. Some use them, but many papers and the AP continue to abbreviate Mississippi as Miss., not MS. States with short names such as Iowa and Maine are never abbreviated. If you're not sure how to handle a particular state, check the *AP Stylebook* under the name of the state. These sentences are correct:

He lives in Oxford, Miss., but works in Tennessee.
He lives in Mississippi but works in Memphis, Tenn.
He thinks Mississippi taxes are lower than Tennessee taxes.

Organization names are trickier. It's a good idea to check the stylebook to determine when to abbreviate them. A few organizations (the FBI, for example) can be abbreviated even the first time you refer to them. However, names of most organizations are spelled out on first reference. On subsequent reference, names of many well-known organizations are abbreviated without periods. The Federal Communications Commission, for example, is spelled out on first reference but called the FCC (no periods) from then on. Assume that this is the first paragraph of a news story:

The FBI is investigating reports that officials of the Federal Communications Commission accepted bribes from people who wanted to acquire TV stations. The FCC is responsible for deciding who can buy broadcast properties.

For most groups, the AP prefers to use generic terms (the committee, the group, the corporation) on subsequent reference. Check with the stylebook to see how to deal with specific organizations. Here are examples of generic references:

The Committee for Clean Air opposes Consolidated Power Corp.'s plan to use the land for industrial development.
The group (*not* "The CCA"), a newly formed coalition of environmental organizations, wants the corporation (*not* "the CPC," unless it is well-known locally) to build its power plants elsewhere.

United States is an exception. It's always spelled out as a noun but abbreviated *U.S.* (with periods) as an adjective:

> Northern State University will offer free correspondence courses to U.S. soldiers overseas but not to troops stationed in the United States. NSU (no periods) students will serve as tutors.

Months are spelled out when an exact date is not given ("in November"). Months with longer names are abbreviated when the exact date is given ("on Nov. 9"). March, April, May, June and July are never abbreviated. Here are some examples:

> In November, he said he would resign from Congress by Dec. 15.
> On Nov. 13, he said he would resign from Congress in December.
> She told reporters in June that she would leave on July 18.

When the month, day and year are given, commas are placed after both the day and the year. When only the month and year or the month and day are given, no commas are used.

> He resigned from Congress on July 12, 1994, and started work in August 1995 with the CIA.
> He resigned from Congress in July 1994 and started work on Aug. 5, 1995, with the CIA.

The only titles abbreviated before names are Dr., Gov., Lt. Gov., Mr., Mrs., Rep., Sen., the Rev. and some military and police titles.

> President Luis Martinez of Mexico and Texas Gov. Armando Cortez toured the site.
> Police Lt. Carl Johnson was assigned to drive Gen. Clinton Booksmith during his tour of the state's Army bases.
> California Sen. Shantel Williams supported the nomination of Attorney General Susan Blackstone of Montana to the Supreme Court.

Only official titles are capitalized. So, *wrestler* and *first baseman* are not capitalized in these sentences:

> Professional wrestler Brick Wall may run for Congress.
> He tossed the ball to first baseman Mike Clampton.

When job descriptions are not used as titles or when they come after a name, they are not abbreviated or capitalized.

> Luis Martinez, the president of Mexico, and Armando Cortez, the governor of Texas, toured the site.
> *or* The president of Mexico, Luis Martinez, and the governor of Texas, Armando Cortez, toured the site.
> Shantel Williams, a Republican senator from California, supported the nomination of Susan Blackstone, Montana's attorney general, to the Supreme Court.
> *or* Sen. Shantel Williams, R-Calif., supported the nomination of the Montana Attorney General Susan Blackstone to the Supreme Court.
> *or* Sen. Shantel Williams, a Republican from California, supported the nomination of the attorney general of Montana, Susan Blackstone, to the Supreme Court.

Titles are not used with names on second reference. Here are two paragraphs from a story:

Judge Harriet Stone ruled that the FBI was not justified in searching the private records of the chairman of the Federal Communications Commission.
Stone (not "Judge Stone") said, "I just don't buy their contention that he left his private records in plain view."

Some papers make one exception to this rule: If several paragraphs separate references to a person, they may use the title to remind readers who the person is.

EXERCISE 6   NAME _____

Practice exercise. Answers in back of book.

This exercise gives you practice in capitalization, abbreviations and other aspects of basic AP style. Don't rewrite the sentences except as needed to make these corrections. Assume that all street addresses are in Northern City, that the paper uses street numbers to identify local residents, and that the paper is published in Northern City, the home of NSU. Names are spelled correctly on first reference.

STORY 1

NSU provost Marcella Jones suspended on Tuesday a History Professor who has been charged with soliciting for prostitution.

Police arrested Prof. Carl J Dow Sunday night at 5th Street and Vine Avenue, an area known for prostitution, after he alledgedly offered a 19 year old police cadet money in exchange for a sex act. City police were conducting an undercover operation along a 12 block segment of Vine Avenue. 34 men and 3 women were arrested on a variety of solicitation and prostitution charges.

According to police records, Dow was convicted of a similar charge in Issaquah, Washington, on December 5th, 1993 and sentenced to thirty hours of community service.

At his arraignment Tuesday, Dow, 43, 367 East 11th Street, pleaded not guilty. His trial is set for April First.

Dow's attorney, Laura Fulton, said Dow told her that he thought the woman was a student in one of his classes and had asked her if she wanted a ride only because she was walking in a bad neighborhood.

Provost Jones said that Dow will be suspended with pay until the matter is settled. She said the University was never informed of his conviction in Washington.

Prof. Dow has taught at the University for ten years and is chair of its 3-year-old Roosevelt Center. He has written 2 books and 15 articles on the history of the United States Navy.

STORY 2

A British professor visiting Northern State University's campus died Tuesday shortly after a car hit him as he walked across N. 9th Street in front of the Science Building, police said.

Dr. John Wilkin, 68, of York, England, was struck about 2:30 PM. He was pronounced dead on arrival at Northern City Hospital.

Two N.S.U. professors walking behind Dr. Wilkins said he looked right instead of left to check for on-coming traffic. He then stepped off the curb in front of a car driven by Billy James Currant, 23, 234 South Eighth Avenue. Vehicles in the United Kingdom drive on the opposite side of the street.

Police said Currant, a Northern State University graduate student in psychology, was not charged. He was treated at Northern City Hospital for shock.

Wilkin, a physicist at the University of York, was in the U.S. visiting other scientists who are doing research in propulsion. He was to address a graduate Physics class Tuesday night and to be the guest of honor at a reception Tuesday night.

EXERCISE 7   NAME _____

This exercise gives you practice in capitalization, abbreviations, spelling and other basics of AP style. Don't rewrite the sentences except as needed to make these corrections. Assume that all street addresses are in Northern City, that the paper uses street numbers to identify local residents and that the paper is published in Northern City, the home of NSU. Names are spelled correctly on first reference.

STORY 1

A Northern State University student driving a car with safety defects was charged with vehicular homicide after a crash Wednesday that killed five of fourteen family members riding in a pickup truck, according to police reports.

The accident at six a.m. on East King Street near North Washington Boulevard injured the other 9 people in the pickup.

Police said N.S.U. student Timothy Douglas, 23, 654 N. 9th Avenue, was driving east on King Street when his car hit the rear of a truck driven by Anthony Smith, 42, 3451 North 8th Avenue.

As many as ten people may have been riding in the covered bed of the pickup, State Police Sargeant Willie Hughes said. All of them were related and ranged in age from 5 to 75. They were traveling from Smith's home to a family reunion at Wilderness Fun Park on North Twelfth Avenue, a distance of about 2 miles. The park charges a five-dollar admission per vehicle.

Sargeant Hughes said Douglas told him that the head lights on his car had not worked for 4 or 5 days but he had not had time to get them fixed. Hughes also said records indicate that Douglas' car failed a state inspection last month because tread on 3 of its 4 tires was worn below legal limits. Hughes said it did not appear Douglas had replaced the tires.

Killed in the crash were Jesse Smith, 39, and his wife, Maria, 34, 423 South Mercy Drive; Sarah O'Day, 34, and her son, Robert, 8, 904 East 9th Ave.; and James Smith, 61, 895 Pine Tree Trail.

The injured included a five-year-old boy and a nine-year-old girl. Both were burned severely over 5 percent of their bodies.

Timothy faces twenty years in jail and fines of up to five-thousand dollars if found guilty of vehicular homicide.

STORY 2

Two masked gunmen posing as under-cover police officers forced their way into a home, tied up a Northern State Professor and her two dinner guests and then ransacked her home Tuesday night.

English Professor Sylvia Malone, 61, said she heard a knock on the door of her home at 5634 W. Treeline Drive at about 8 p.m. One of the men flashed a police badge and then kicked open the door. Both home invaders wore black clothes and had black hoods over their faces.

The men robbed two dinner guests, NSU sociology professor Maggie LeConte, 212 South Maple Drive, and Dr. Carlos Maunez, 5438 Silver Avenue. They took a small medical bag that Maunez, an orthopedic surgeon, carries with him. They also took Professor Malone's laptop computer and a small amount of cash before fleeing in Maunez's white Porsche 911. The car has a vanity license plate reading BONE-FIXER.

Police asked anyone with information about the crime or who has seen the car to call the department's Crimeline at 555-TIPS.

SECTION 4: CHECKING WORD USAGE AND GRAMMAR IN THE *AP STYLEBOOK*

We've used the AP Stylebook for information and for rulings on when to abbreviate and capitalize words. However, the stylebook serves another major role in the life of copy editors: It's a convenient, straightforward guide to many common word usage, grammar and punctuation problems.

Occasionally, you will find that the AP's rules on grammar and word usage are at odds with what you see in novels and textbooks. On occasion, the AP will even disagree with your English teachers. Unlike some languages, English has no governing body that dictates what is correct. That means authorities can disagree. Also, English is in a constant state of flux. New words are added, and the meanings of some older words change.

Nevertheless, newspapers want consistency. They want all reporters to follow the same rules, so newspapers expect reporters and editors to abide by the stylebook.

In this section of the workbook, we give you exercises that will allow you to become familiar with the *AP Stylebook* rules on grammar, usage and word meanings. We go through the book systematically. The first exercises cover the material in the stylebook's *A* and *B* sections; the final exercise emphasizes *T* through *Z*.

What's the best way to do these exercises? We suggest that you skim the designated sections of the stylebook first. You'll probably discover lots of facts about English that you never imagined. Then go through the stories trying to find all the errors. It's not as simple as looking up every word that begins with *A* or *B*. For example, suppose that you're editing this sentence: "He effected the lives of many people." If you wanted to check whether "effected" is the right word, you'd find the answer in the *A* section under "affect." Before each exercise, there's a quick review of the section covered. The answers are in the back of the book.

We've also included errors in basic grammar and style: capitalization, numbers and abbreviations. So you may need to check material either in the basic style section of this workbook or in the stylebook. After we introduce a problem, we may repeat it in later exercises.

We have written these exercises to give you practice in applying the rules in the *AP Stylebook*. Don't rewrite the sentences, although most of them need rewriting. Just correct the grammar, punctuation, word usage and so on.

EXERCISE 8: QUICK REVIEW OF THE A AND B SECTIONS   NAME _____

Practice exercise. Answers in back of book.

1. The reporter could not (accept, except) the free ticket.
2. The (affects, effects) of the draught were severe in rural areas, but residents of urban areas were not (affected, effected).
3. The Senate (approved, passed) a bill making it illegal to fly hot-air balloons in (adverse, averse) weather.
4. Her son is (five, 5) years old, an (aid, aide) to the mayor said.
5. Police charged the (nineteen-year-old) (19-year-old) with (allegedly, nothing) stealing the car.
6. Karl Schmidt, an (alumnus, alumni) of North High School, was given the award by (Acting, acting) (Mayor, mayor) Cindy Voelz.
7. He divided the candy (among, between) his five children.
8. Police were armed with shotguns because the chief (anticipated, expected) trouble.
9. The (arbitrator, mediator) will decide who gets the car.
10. The young man was (arrested for, arrested on a charge of) killing his father.
11. An average of 500 students (is, are) given parking tickets each week.
12. The average cost of a house in that area (is, are) $120,000.
13. Nearly all the students in the class of ('02, 02) received (As, A's) in math.
14. He wanted to (back up, backup) his computer disk before the (back yard, backyard) cookout.
15. The liberal (bloc, block) of the party supports the tax increase.
16. Police investigated the (break in, break-in, breakin) of (four, 4) parked school (buses, busses).

EXERCISE 9   NAME _____

Practice exercise. Answers in back of book.

You'll find the correct usage for many of the errors in this exercise in the A and B sections of the AP Stylebook. Don't revise or rewrite the exercise—or any of the exercises in this section—except to make needed style and grammar corrections. Because this is a practice exercise, an edited version is in the back of the book. Assume that the story is for a paper in the city where NSU is. In all exercises, assume the names are correct on first reference. Make sure that the names and facts are consistent.

Northern State University officials may have to turn down $900,000 left to the university because of the unusual demands the donor made, according to Northern State Pres. Richard Aster.

To receive the money, N.S.U. must rename their Political Science Department in honor of a man arrested for allegedly trying to blow up an army base in Florida during World War II.

The grant is part of a $10,000,000 gift being offered to several universities by Dr. Homer Schmidt, a Charleston, Illinois, internist who ran for President of the United States 4 times on a variety of antiwar tickets in the 1960s and '70s.

Dr. Schmidt's will specified how the money is to be divided between ten universities and gave detailed instructions for its use. If any university turns down the grant, their money will be added to the gifts to the other universities.

An aid to Governor Alonzo Childres said the Governor first learned of the will Tuesday. Gov. Childres said he had asked University officials to consider the donor's background before excepting the money. Since it is a private gift to NSU, the Governor cannot order the university to refuse it.

Pres. Astor said NSU officials also feared averse reactions from the public. "I'm afraid changing the name of the department might effect the image of Northern State University in the community," he said. "We can't be sure what effect something like this might have." He said he had appointed a three-man committee to review the proposal and had asked Vice President Martha Boone to chair it.

The NSU Faculty Senate Tuesday passed a resolution opposing the measure. They had all ready passed an amendment to their bylaws requiring their approval of name changes on campus.

Etta Cunning, President of the Faculty Senate, said sentiment on campus is against the gift. "You just can't name departments after any one that gives the school a bunch of money," she said.

Prof. Cunning said she knew Schmidt and anticipated that he might leave money to the school. However, she said she had no idea what restrictions he would place on the money and had made no plans for how to handle the gift.

Dr. Schmidt's will requires NSU to name its political science department after Clarence Wilson, an alumni of the university. Wilson was arrested for alleged treason and attempted murder in 1942 after a bomb allegedly exploded near a Army troop train in Panacea, Florida. The charges were later dropped.

The will also established a scholarship fund at NSU and specified the first 4 recipients. They were Mark White, 19, 1459 South Park Avenue, Mary Williams, 20, 120 North Fifth Street, Clyde Overdorf, 32, 2315 West Johnson Drive, and Sidney Jones, 22, 234 East Twelfth Avenue. The will says that future scholarship must be given "to brave students who fight the system."

EXERCISE 10   NAME _____

Mistakes in this exercise are based on material in the basic style section (Section 3) of this workbook and correlate to the *A* and *B* sections of the *AP Stylebook*. Don't revise or rewrite the story. But do correct the errors in style, punctuation and word usage. Make sure that names and facts are consistent. Assume that the story is for a paper in the same city as NSU. In all exercises, assume that the paper follows the custom of cleaning up minor grammar errors when quoting sources and that names are correct on first reference.

Police arrested a 26 year old Northern State University police officer on Monday for shooting to death another campus police officer during an off duty quarrel.

Patrolman John R. Grant was charged with allegedly killing Detective Craig Devon Cargal, 32.

According to police reports, Grant was sitting in a car belonging to Ashley Aldajuste, 20, 3254 North Tenth Avenue parked behind the Kmart on West Colonial Boulevard at about 2 a.m. Monday morning.

Aldajuste said Cargal, whom she described as a former boyfriend walked up to the car and asked her to leave with him. When she refused the two men started fighting.

Aldajuste told police Grant pulled a gun and shot Cargal. She helped detectives find a .22-caliber revolver on the roof of Whitney's Tires For Less, 341 South East Street. The gun which was not his service handgun was registered to Grant.

"I thought things were alright between me and Craig," Aldojuste told police. "Then this had to happen. He couldn't leave well enough alone. He knew John and me were already talking about marriage."

Grant, 26, turned himself into police at noon Monday. He is being held without bail on charges of second degree murder. Since the shooting involved a police officer, the department will ask state officials to handle the investigation.

Cargal was in his tenth year on the force. He spent four years as an undercover officer investigating drug rings before becoming a detective. Grant joined the force last year.

Each of the officers were honored at a banquet in December. Cargal was cited for his work in the arrest of a man who robbed the NSU Credit Union office on campus. Grant received the Mayor's Badge of Bravery for rescuing a four-year-old girl from a burning car.

N.S.U. Police Chief Cordell Morris said the incident had left his department deeply saddened. "The officers are taking this hard," he said. "It's a real tragedy for everyone involved. Greg Cargal was a hard worker and was well liked. Grant was new on the force but had a solid record. I don't know what effect this is going to have on our officers, but I know it has effected me deeply."

Cargal's arrest Monday was the latest incident involving the problem riddled department. Last year two officers were convicted of receiving payoffs from a drug ring that was operating on campus. They are now serving ten year terms in a state prison.

The NSU campus biweekly newspaper said in a front page story Monday that their sources believe NSU President Richard Aster may break-up the department if it receives any more adverse publicity.

"We can't allow any part of the university to tarnish the reputation of the university as a whole," the paper quoted Aster as telling aids. "Either the department chiefs will effect changes to the program or I will show them the door."

The student run paper is publishing a three-part series on the department's problems. At a press conference, Chief Morris alluded to the series, which began in last week's papers. He said student journalists who are anti-police wrote the stories.

EXERCISE 11   NAME _____

Quick check of the C section. Answers in back of book.

1. The (Mayor, mayor) was in an accident at Main and State (Streets, streets, sts.).
2. The U.S. (Capitol, Capital) is the most impressive building in Washington.
3. The Republican and Democratic (Parties, parties) refused to (cave-in, cave in) on the issue.
4. (Charleston, Charlestown) is the (capitol, capital) of West Virginia.
5. (Church-goers, Churchgoers) will try to (clean-up, cleanup, clean up) the city's corrupt police department.
6. The (co-author, coauthor) of the bill said he would (co-operate, cooperate) with Republicans and (co-ordinate, coordinate) its support in the Senate.
7. Purdue lost (its, their) tourney opener, but the Cardinals won (its, their) game by 20 points.
8. The council decided to end (their, its) meeting with a prayer.
9. After he paid her a (complement, compliment) on her singing, she gave him a (complementary, complimentary) ticket to her next concert.
10. Lincoln hoped (Congress, congress) would pay the soldiers.
11. The lawyer said he has studied the (Constitution, constitution), and he sees no real (Constitutional, constitutional) problem with the law.
12. She compared her editor (with, to) a drunken baboon.
13. She contrasted the Democrat's proposal (with, to) the Republican bill.
14. Boone was convicted (of, for) selling heroin in Celina (comma, no comma) (Tennessee, Tenn.) (comma, no comma) and Glascow (comma, no comma) (Kentucky, Ky.) (comma, no comma) last year.
15. The lawyer tried to (convince, persuade) the jury that no (copywrite, copyright) laws were broken.
16. The corporation's lawyer tried to (convince, persuade) the judge to allow compensatory damages.
17. The (cover up, cover-up, coverup) was meant to hide (cut backs, cutbacks) in housing allowances in order to (cut off, cutoff) Bradley's main source of support.

EXERCISE 12   NAME _____

The following story emphasizes the "C" section of the *AP Stylebook* and repeats material from earlier exercises. The sentences may have grammar and punctuation problems. Fix these problems, but don't do any other rewriting. Assume that it's for the same paper as the previous exercise.

Northern State University football coach Truman Marshall tried to convince the college's Faculty Senate Wednesday that they should not stop three football players, who were arrested for burglary Sunday, from playing in Saturday's game against Buckley College.

The players, all starters on this years undefeated team, pleaded not guilty Monday and were released on bond. They have been practicing with the team this week.

Saturdays game is important for the Blasters who are undefeated. They can wrap up their first conference title in 22 years by defeating Buckley. Buckley has also won all of their conference games.

Truman told a special meeting of the faculty senate that he does not believe the college can keep the trio from playing Saturday. "They have been found guilty of nothing," he said. "They haven't even been tried yet. The university is violating a cannon of American justice. We don't punish people in America until they are found guilty."

"The university should treat athletes just as it would any other students, Truman continued, I think we would give any other student the benefit of the doubt."

Etta Cunning, President of the Faculty Senate, disagreed. She urged Senators to pass a resolution barring any student charged with a felony from participating in any university related activity.

"The reputation of a school is based in part on the character of its student body," she said. She said she did not want to see Northern State compared to 'football factories where winning is the only thing.' Cunning is a Professor in the History Department.

After ninety minutes of discussion, the senate voted, 18-3, to appoint a three man committee to study the charges, interview the players and report to the Senate Friday. Cunningham will chair the committee.

NSU President Richard Aster told the senate that the university will take whatever steps they recommend. "Its a decision that representatives of the university faculty should make."

Police arrested the players Saturday night after an apartment in the Spanish Trace complex was allegedly broken-into. Backup quarterback Sam Whitehead, 21, 2314 East Triplet Drive, and starting center Dwight Long, 19, 234 North Bumby Avenue, were arrested at Amesville Clinic where they had gone for treatment of cuts they received when they broke a window to get into the apartment.

Dewey Rich, a 22-year-old all-conference linebacker, was arrested after his car collided with a telephone pole at Fifth Ave. and Wilson St. about 5 blocks from the apartment complex. Rich had hidden a stereo he had stolen from the apartment under some blankets in the back seat of his car.

Truman told reporters after meeting with the faculty senate that he would ask Sandy Bennett, a well known criminal attorney, to represent the players. He said Bennett planned to ask a judge to enjoin the university from keeping the players on the sidelines Saturday. Bennett could not be reached by reporters. His secretary said he was in Decatur Illinois for a legal conference.

EXERCISE 13   NAME _____

Quick check of *D, E* and *F* sections. Answers in back of book.

PART 1

1. A (die hard, die-hard, diehard) Knicks fan, he hoped they would draft a (seven footer, 7 footer, 7-footer)
2. Parts of the (East, east) were buried under (two, 2) feet of snow before the storm headed (North, north) into Canada.
3. The mayor and her lover tried to be (discrete, discreet).
4. The children (dived, dove) into the new ($10 thousand, $10,000) pool.
5. Johnson went from (door to door, door-to-door) trying to raise money for the (rundown, run-down) school.
6. The (countdown, count-down) was stopped when a (drunk, drunken) pilot flew too close.
7. Each of the astronauts (was, were) required to leave the Shuttle.
8. Many American teens (emigrated, immigrated) to Canada.
9. The (engine, motor) fell off the jet plane.
10. To (ensure, insure) secrecy, he sealed the letter in an (envelop, envelope).
11. (Everyday, Every day) the private detective spies on peoples' (extramarital, extra-marital) affairs. (Everyone, Every one) says he has a bad job.
12. The station manager was not (fazed, phased) by criticisms from (federal, Federal) regulators.
13. The university library has (fewer, less) books than it should have.
14. She was carrying (fewer, less) than $20 in her purse when she was robbed.
15. The (firefighter, fireman) said a (flair, flare) was used to start the blaze.
16. The man was charged with (first degree, first-degree) murder.
17. In the (first quarter, first-quarter) Jones showed he had a (flair, flare) for rugby.
18. The doctor refused to answer the (follow up, followup, follow-up) question about the safety of (French, french) fries and (Swiss, swiss) cheese.
19. The (front page, front-page) story was written by a writer who had never been to the (front line, front-line, frontline) and worked for the paper (part time, part-time, parttime).
20. His (fund raising, fund-raising, fundraising) abilities led to a (full time, full-time, fulltime) job.

PART 2

Correct any dangling modifiers in these sentences.

1. Waiting for the ambulance to arrive, the pain grew intense and he thought he would die.

2. Missing for three days, police found the girl's body lying in a pool of blood.

3. Gliding effortlessly over the water, the Hovercraft is an efficient ferry.

4. After receiving more than $1 million in campaign contributions, reporters believed Johnson was

   unbeatable.

PART 3

Punctuate these sentences correctly.

1. Darryl Johnson who won Saturday's race was later disqualified.

2. Officials said he had used a gasoline additive that had been outlawed.

3. Bill's Meat Market which sold the spoiled meat has been sued by three parents whose children suffered food poisoning.

EXERCISE 14   NAME _____

The following story emphasizes the *D, E,* and *F* sections of the *AP Stylebook* and repeats material from earlier exercises. The sentences may have grammar and punctuation problems. Fix them, but don't do any other rewriting.

Having pulled the program from the brink of disaster, Coach Maurice Collins leads his Northern State University basketball team tonight into their first season as a full fledged basketball power.

Most of the excitement is being generated by two 7-footers in the Blasters' line-up, Andre and Maurice Biengot from Avignon, France. The pair has dazzled fans in preseason games with their deft touch from the perimeter and their monstrous slam dunks. Between them, they averaged 61 points and 21 rebounds in the teams three preseason exhibition games

The Beingots have also brought a new cheer to Barr Memorial Fieldhouse. Since their last name is pronounced bee-en-go the NSU bench began to yell 'Bingo' when the players scored. The cheer caught on with Blaster fans.

Even Basketball Week, a national sports magazine referred to the Blasters 'Bingo offense' They predicted that if the Beingot brothers stay healthy the Blasters will win the conference title and make their first appearance in the NCAA tourney.

Sportswriters from 120 media outlets will be in the NSU field house to get their first-look at the brothers in regular season play. The game has been sold-out for two months.

The presence of the Biengot brothers is just one of Collins' accomplishments in his 5 years at the helm of the Blasters.

When he took over the program, it was foundering. Although 60000 people often packed Weyger Stadium for Blaster football games, most fans decided to forgo the basketball Blasters and its continual string of losing seasons. The program reached its lowpoint when less than 100 people bought season tickets for the 98-99 season. NSU's average of 1800 paid admissions was the lowest in their conference that season.

Collins quickly brought new excitement to Blaster basketball. He was different than previous NSU basketball coaches. He had a flare for publicity and was a natural showman who often flouted his career as an NBA player. The NSU program started to get front page coverage in most area newspapers.

Collins was far-sighted enough to recognize that without a superior center, he could never draw fans to the arena and do the kind of fundraising the program needed. Upon taking the job, the search for a first-class center became his top priority.

While on vacation in France, Collins ran into Carl Winters, an NSU alumni. Winters raved to Collins about a seven foot four teen-ager, he had seen playing basketball at a tiny Christian school near Avignon Winter convinced Collins that he should take the 3 hour train ride to see the player.

Collins said could not believe his eyes as he watched Maurice Biengot play in a pickup game in a village in France's Provence region. Collins said the teen seemed literally to explode off the ground and dunk the ball. Collins was even more impressed when he saw the player consistently sink baskets from the backcourt. The further he stood from the rim, Collins said, the more effortless his shots became. Collins said he and Winters looked at one another and smiled.

"But it isn't Maurice that I want you to see" Winters said, Its his brother I wanted you to see. He's a little taller and quicker."

That evening Collins met Maurice's taller brother Andre and their parents. Knowing that he couldn't let this chance pass by, information about NSU was quickly given to the players. Then Collins' hopes were temporarily dashed. Bridget Biengot, the boy's mother, did not want them to live in the U.S., so far from home. Each of the youths was enrolled in a local technical college. But the brothers persuaded her that they would get a better education in computer science by attending an American school.

Since NCAA and university admissions deadlines were fewer than two weeks away Collins contacted U.S. Senator Woodrow Emerson who asked Federal officials to rush the paperwork. NSU Provost Marcella Jones herself processed the brothers' entrance applications, and tonight they'll lead the Blasters into the team's most promising season ever.

EXERCISE 15: QUICK REVIEW OF
SECTIONS G THROUGH L   NAME _____

Answers in back of book.

1. The (9th-graders, ninth-graders) seem much younger than the (tenth-graders 10th graders).
2. Even a group of doctors (was, were) appalled by the (grisly, grizzly) scene.
3. He made a (half-hearted, halfhearted) effort to pass the (half-baked, halfbaked) bill.
4. Sue (hanged, hung) the (hand-made, handmade) rug on the wall.
5. He went to his (home-town, hometown, home town) to (hold-up, holdup, hold up) a bank.
6. The miners (suffered, received) several injuries in the (cave in, cave-in, cavein).
7. "(It's, Its) time to move on," the mayor said. "The race has run (it's, its) course."
8. The corporation lost (its, it's, their) suit against the (Federal, federal) (Government, government).
9. The gunman ordered the customers to (lie, lay) on the floor.
10. The company (layed, laid, lay) off 500 workers last week.
11. The body was (laying, lying) in the street when police arrived.
12. (Senator, Sen.) Bob White and (Representative, Rep.) Sue Jones spoke next.
13. The reporters were told to limit the number of (long-distance, long distance) calls.

EXERCISE 16   NAME _____

The following story emphasizes sections *G* through *L* in the *AP Stylebook* and repeats material from earlier exercises. The sentences may have grammar, spelling and punctuation problems. Fix them, but don't do any other rewriting. Make the same assumptions as on earlier exercises. Assume that your newspaper identifies people by age and exact address.

Prosecutors told a grisly tale of the execution style murder of two Northern City policemen Monday as the trial of two prominent Northern City men got underway.

John Wilson Jr., age 32, 223 South Brook Drive and Harry Smith, age 40, 344 East 5th Avenue, are charged with killing the officers, Clyde Brickston, 23, and Sarah Goodwife, 21. Wilson is a professor of business administration at Fort Gibson Community College and Smith is president of Higher International, an alleged importing firm in Longwood.

In his opening remarks state's attorney Hamilton Morrow said Wilson and Smith are the masterminds of a local drug operation which killed the police officers. The jury of five men and seven women were quite as Hamilton showed them graphic pictures of the murder victims.

"If we just sit back and keep a hands-off policy toward drugs then nobody will be safe" Hamilton said "These murders were the result of gorilla warfare being waged by drug dealers in our city."

Hamilton said that the two patrol officers were investigating a one-car accident on a deserted section of North Tenth Street near McKinley Avenue. Smith had lost control of a car he was driving and it collided with a telephone pole. Smiths head had hit the steering wheel and he was bleeding badly from the nose and mouth.

As Goodwife tried to aide Smith, she saw a small plastic bag filled with a white powder in his front shirt pocket. When Wilson, a passenger in Smith's car, saw Goodwife reaching for the bag he pointed a pistol at Goodwife and ordered both officers to lay on the ground.

According to the prosecutor, Wilson then shot each of them in the back of the head with a high powered shotgun. They ran from the scene but were captured by police a few minutes later.

He said "I will produce a witness, who will testify that the killers teased the officers as they laid on the ground and laughed as if its a big joke to kill cops".

Hamilton warned the jury not to be deceived by the mens appearance. "They may wear suits and ties," he said, "but there nothing more than street punks".

Hamilton held up a brochure, which claimed that Higher International specialized in importing hard to get South American candies. "Who do they think they are kidding" Hamilton asked. "We all know what they mean by the word "candy", don't we?".

Hamilton accused Smith and Wilson of having ties to Carlos Hernandez who was convicted in May 1994 of running the largest drug operation in the state. Hernandez last year kidnaped a guard and escaped while he was being transferred from a Federal prison in Joliet, Illinois to a maximum security facility in Terre Haute Indiana.

Defense Attorneys Omar Braddle and Gene Quincy interrupted Hamilton several times. They asked judge Martha White to limit Hamilton's comments to the case under consideration. "He's trying them for crimes they haven't been charged with," Braddle said. "Its not fair."

However, the Judge, a former police officer rejected each of their pleas.

Defense Attorneys also complained that flags in front of the city police station have remained at half mast in memory of the murdered policemen. "Everyday jurors on their way to the courthouse see those flags," Quincy said. Judge White refused their request to have the flags flown at their normal height.

In an unusual statement before the day's session the Judge warned newspapers to be more responsible in their coverage of the trial and inferred that she would not be averse to moving the trial to another county.

The trial has attracted considerable attention because of the prominence of the defendants. There's been two large rallies staged by an antidrug group which wants police to clean-up the city.

EXERCISE 17: QUICK REVIEW OF
THE M THROUGH O SECTIONS   NAME _____

Answers in back of book.

1. A majority of the voters (is, are) undecided.
2. The town (marshal, marshall) found the letter on the fireplace (mantel, mantle).
3. The sociologist said, "Even the (middle class, middle-class) is beginning to reject traditional (middle class, middle-class) values."
4. (General, Gen.) Lou Black said the new tanks must go 40 (m.p.h., mph).
5. The (General, general) approved the ($3,000,000, $3 million) project.
6. Three people died in the (accident, mishap).
7. The coach said the Panthers will try to (mix up, mix-up) the Detroit (Lion's, Lions') defense.
8. Neither the (Lions, Lion's) nor their coach (is, are) predicting victory.
9. The (multi-millionaire, multimillionaire) is from (Mount, Mt.) Vernon.
10. None of the players (is, are) very talented, and none of the coaches (agree, agrees) on who will start.
11. In a (three-to-two, 3 to 2, 3–2) decision, the court ruled that more than (two, 2) public defenders should have represented the (ten, 10) (protesters, protestors).
12. The accident was at (Tenth, 10th) Avenue and (Second, 2nd) Street.
13. After a big (send off, send-off, sendoff) at the airport, the team will (stop off, stop-off, stopoff) in Brooklyn before going to the (play offs, playoffs, play-offs).
14. Investigators said the (flameout, flame-out) was caused by (outdated, out-dated) parts being installed in the jet's engine.
15. During a (stop over, stop-over, stopover) in Paris, a passenger tried to (takeover, take-over, take over) the bus.
16. Seeing that the child was dead, (tears filled the firefighter's eyes, the firefighter fought back tears.)

EXERCISE 18   NAME _____

The following story emphasizes sections *M* through *O* in the *AP Stylebook* and repeats material from earlier exercises. The sentences may have grammar, spelling and punctuation problems. Fix them, but don't do any other rewriting.

An American lawyer who was kidnapped by Columbian drug smugglers, told reporters that for the past 8 months he assumed everyday would be his last.

Carl E. Johnson, laying safely in a hospital bed aboard a U.S. Navy ship, described his dramatic escape to reporters.

Johnson said he was in Colombia representing the Allison Chemical Corporation in their efforts to recover $6,000,000 the company says the Colombian government owes for pesticides bought in early 90's.

Johnson said he was gathering information in a rural village when a gang of teen-aged gunmen captured him. They lead him to a near-by camp where they showed-off their prize to military officers.

However, many of the leaders wanted nothing to do with a captured American and argued that they should kill Johnson. But one youth convinced them that they should keep him alive long enough to get millions of dollars in ransom from the U.S. government and the Allison company.

After deciding to keep him alive for awhile, Johnson was locked away in a storage closet at a drug processing plant.

Johnson said his opportunity to escape came when a drunken guard tried to attack him. He said he slugged the guard causing his knife to flip out of his hand and skip across the floor until it lay no more than inches form his feet.

Johnson said he grabbed the knife and then layed the unconscience guard in his bunk and put on the man's clothes. He then sat near the door of his cell, and planned his escape. Following a regular pattern, he knew his captors would spend the morning loading drugs into trucks.

When the trucks pulled into the camp he waited a couple of minutes and then walked from his cell. Considerably less men were in the camp than he had expected, and they were too busy loading the truck to notice as he walked out of the camp.

About 2 hours later his ordeal ended. He saw two multi-colored busses full of American tourists less than 10 miles from the camp. When the driver stopped he persuaded him that he was an American citizen.

"I think he thought I was lieing, but he didn't know what else to do so he let me on bus. The other Americans believed my story and convinced the driver that he should take me to the U.S. embassy," Johnson said.

Johnson said his kidnapers kept him in a small closet and gave him only a fifteen minute break in the mornings to get some exercise.

"I kept my sanity by playing child-like games," he said. He said he was afraid he would go mad if he just lay in bed all day thinking about his situation.

Johnson will arrive in Dalton, Georgia, his home town, at 12 noon Friday. The Governor of Georgia, William Dodge, and other dignitaries will be on hand to welcome him back.

EXERCISE 19: QUICK REVIEW OF
THE P THROUGH R SECTIONS   NAME _____

Answers in back of book.

SECTION 1

1. A story on (page four, page 4, Page 4) said that the child's death was reported on (page one, Page One, Page 1) of his hometown paper.
2. (Senator, Sen.) Caroline Jackson, [R-Minn. (R-Minn.)], got her husband a (part time, part-time, parttime) job in the Pentagon.
3. The reporter was told he could not work (part time, part-time, parttime) for the Republican (party, Party).
4. He said (four, 4) (percent, per cent, %) of the population (was, were) without food, and (seventy, 70) (percent, per cent, %) of the roads (was, were) destroyed.
5. Halfway through the trial, the attorney asked what the charge against his client was (period, ?)
6. The salesman (persuaded, convinced) the young man to give him his car keys.
7. The attorney (persuaded, convinced) the judge that the salesman was a thief.
8. The next day, the salesman (plead, pleaded, pled) guilty.
9. Teams from three local (churchs, churches) will be in the (play-offs, playoffs, play offs).
10. The (principal, principle) reason the school board fired the high school (principal, principle) was that he had violated the ethical (principals, principles) of the community.
11. (Professor, Prof.) Mike Moses was held in the county (prison, jail) until he became sober.
12. According to the (profile, pro-file) in the paper, Smith was (prolabor, pro-labor) all his life.
13. (Passers-by, Passer-bys) said the (attorney generals, attorneys general) were chatting amiably.
14. The Green Bay Packers (ravaged, ravished) Bengal quarterback Sam Dawkins.
15. The liberals feared (rightwingers, right-wingers, right wingers) would take over the (Party, party).
16. The mayor said she would not (second guess, second-guess) the police chief's decision to buy (second hand, second-hand, secondhand) firearms.
17. He owned a (second rate, second-rate, secondrate) resort on a (semi-tropical, semitropical) island.
18. The (spokesman, spokesperson) said he could not answer the question.

SECTION 2

Assume the correct spellings of names are Bill Jones and Judy Schultz. Follow the AP's style rules (which at places are different from those of other style manuals).

1. Bill Jones daughter won an award in Judy Schultzs speech class.
2. Tuesdays paper said that the Legislature plans to cut the Northern State University budget.
3. The attorney generals of Maine and Iowa filed reports with the presidents legal staff.
4. Five police officers saw the incident. The officers statements differed. One officers report said he found cocaine hidden in the mans pants. Two of the officers reports said they found cocaine in the womens purses.
5. The Jones came to the concert, but the Whites decided to go to the party. Their childrens babysitter had to be home by 11 PM.
6. Five citys plan to sue the county over its plans to reduce patrols by deputies within the cities. Its the first time a city has sued the county.
7. The professor said that Marxs philosophy is much like Jesuses philosophy.
8. The event is for 7 and 8 year olds.

SECTION 3

Check the spelling of these words. (Dictionaries may list alternative spellings. Most newspapers use the AP's spelling.)

refered	controled	totaled	quarreled	backwards	offered
canceled	refering	totaling	sizable	quized	modeled
abused	combating	omited	reoccuring	hauled	occured
alloted	confered	reoccured	alledged	towards	
bused to school					

EXERCISE 20   NAME _____

The following exercise adds the *S* section but also continues to emphasize sections *P* through *R* in the *AP Stylebook* and repeats material from earlier exercises. The sentences may have grammar, spelling and punctuation problems. Fix these errors, but don't do any other rewriting.

SECTION 1

Correct spelling and grammar errors in the following sentences. Assume that the names are spelled Bill Jones and Paula White.

1. Bill Jones son wore shorts and a t-shirt to Paula Whites party. His friends wore suits and ties.

2. The nations cities are declining, the senators aide said, while the president is out politicing in the primaries.

3. She used her mothers money to attend a teachers college in Iowa only to learn its difficult for women to get a teaching job in higher education.

4. Cleveland and Toledo asked the census bureau to change the way its workers count transients. These citys populations are falling rapidly and they want the transients counted as residents so their share of federal aid will not be reduced.

5. This years census found more people living in poverty than ever before. It also found declines in the number of citizens in the middle and upper income brackets.

SECTION 2

Edit these stories for style errors, bad grammar and misspellings.

STORY 1

Senator Carl Morris (D-Illinois) asked congress Wednesday who stopped the shipment of supplies to the flood victims in Mexico?

Morris said, "I could not believe the United States would lay down on the job when it comes to helping friendly nations. Its a basic principle of American life that we help our neighbors. And its time we started to do something about it."

Officials of a Federal task force organizing aide for Mexican flood victims admitted that they had encountered more problems than expected.

"The storm has destroyed most of the principle highways in the area one worker said. How can we get trucks through."

The problems in south western Mexico began when Spring rains flooded the regions rivers. Rampaging waters completely destroyed five towns and ravished much of the countryside.

At one point the surging Rio Balsas River shutdown the principal highway between Mexico City and Acapulco. The tops of some bridges were hidden under the currents of the swollen river.

U. N. workers estimated that ten per cent of the regions population have been left homeless.

"Why aren't we getting that aid to them" Morris asked? He said the nation must "rally around the sufferring Mexicans or no one in the Central and South America will ever respect us."

Speaking in a nearly-empty Senate hearing room, Morris said a girl from his office had flown over the disaster area and he said that her report brought tears to his eyes. He said she called it the worst flooding she had seen since the Midwestern floods in the sixties.

Trying to rally congressional support, pictures of storm damaged buildings and starving children were given to the senators and reporters by Morrisons staff.

STORY 2

Republican Senator Claude LaRose of New Jersey Tuesday accused Vice-President Marilou Grimes of "spending too much time politicing and not enough time attending to the job of being President of the Senate."

LaRose said he and Senator John Tompkins (D-Oregon) had layed a proposal on Grimes desk two weeks ago. A LaRose aid said it was still laying there unread.

"I think the leader of our Party ought to be out there pedalling our proposals," La Rose said. "Noone is a bigger fan of the President and Vice-President than I am. And I think it is a priviledge to serve under them. But they need to get busy."

LaRose and Tompkins proposal would provide Federal help to identify the principal needs of the nations cities and to aide mayors in solving their problems. Tompkins decided to support LaRose after he heard Senator Homer Harris speech about the problems in Cleveland.

"Its very upsetting when you learn that welfare protestors have become so desperate that they set fire to three policemens homes," he explained. "The more I pore over reports coming from the inner cities, the more I recognize that my Christian principles require me to do whatever I can to aid those people."

Both senators said they believed they could persuade the Senate to adopt a law which would grant five million dollars to the cities. Their proposal would require the cities to repay the grant at an interest rate of only five percent.

More than 60 cities would be eligible for the grants which would be given on a first come first served basis. A supervisory board will funnel the money to residents, who lived in the lower or middle class areas of the cities.

EXERCISE 21: QUICK REVIEW OF
THE T THROUGH Z SECTIONS   NAME _____

Answers in back of book.

1. The terrorists tried to (take over, take-over, takeover) the plane shortly after (take off, take-off, take-off).

2. Horton attended a (teacher's college, teachers college) in Indiana.

3. (Tonights, Tonight's) game will be (telecast, televised) live at (9, 9:00) (PM, p.m. nothing).

4. The temperature at game time was (minus, –) (five, 5) although (higher, warmer) temperatures are expected by halftime.

5. The mayor proposed (that, nothing) the City Council raise taxes. He said (that, nothing) the city needed to repave dozens of streets.

6. The (presidents, president's) speech will begin at (9, 9:00) (PM, P.M., p.m., pm)

7. At the meeting were (Sen., Senator, senator) Suzanne Copeland, (Prof., Professor, professor) Saad al-Juraid and (Oil Baron, oil baron) Luke Potter.

8. The (hold up, hold-up, holdup) man robbed the (walk up, walk-up, walkup) window.

9. The mom told the boy to (clean up, clean-up, cleanup) his room like a (grown up, grown-up, grownup).

10. A biker wearing a (tee shirt, t-shirt, T-shirt) did a (u turn, u-turn, U-turn) on the Interstate.

11. The (vice president, vice-president) of the (U.S., United States) is president of the (senate, Senate).

12. The (four-pound, four pound, 4 pound, 4-pound) baby will be kept in intensive care until it weighs (six-pounds, six pounds, 6 pounds, 6-pounds).

13. The injured man sued the clerk (who, whom, that) sold him the beer.

14. Police have been unable to identify the baby (who, whom) was left in the rest room.

15. The detective wanted to find (whoever, whomever) owned the snake.

16. (Whoever, Whomever) the snake bit will need medical treatment.

17. After a (year-long, yearlong, year long) investigation, the accountant said he found evidence of (wrong-doing, wrongdoing) in the company's (yearend, year-end) reports for each of the (last, past) five years.

EXERCISE 22   NAME _____

These exercises emphasize the *T* through *Z* sections of the *AP Stylebook* and repeat material from earlier exercises.

PART 1

This story has **grammar and punctuation** problems. Fix them, but don't do any other rewriting. Assume that Jacksonville is in your state and that names are correct on first reference.

JACKSONVILLE—Consolidated Software has named Keith Steinberg, a 20 year veteran of the company, to be its new President and Chief Operating Officer. Tuesdays announcement came after a year-long search to replace retiring president Josh Winters.

The Jacksonville based corporation is the nations largest manufacturer of statistical programs and produces several financial packages for home use.

The appointment of Steinberg surprised many industry analysts. The list of people that had been considered for the post, included many of the top names in the computer industry.

The announcement also caught Consolidate's public relations department off guard. They had not been told to prepare materials about Steinbergh Tuesday morning. Secretaries were busy xeroxing his resume as the board was announcing their decision at a press conference.

In a major re-structuring of Consolidate's, leadership, the board of directors also announced that Sydney Ward, the current vice-president in charge of development, will become the company's Chief Financial Officer.

Josh Winters whose father founded the company as a data processing firm in the 70s said he welcomed the boards decision to promote talent from within the organization.

"We need someone as president who knows the company and who can upgrade it's financial systems" Winters said. "Syd Ward can do that. And nobody knows our software better than Keith Steinberg."

Ward will be oversee the companys management, marketing, manufacturing and financial operations and Steinberg, a well regarded engineer who designed the Consolidateds best selling statistics program in the 80's, will remain as director of software development.

Steinberg said the problems facing Consolidated are not much different than the other major software companies are facing.

"The competition is fierce, he said, its a tough time for the software industry. Everyone is constantly having to upgrade their programs to keep up with the capabilities of the new processing chips.

But we're successful because we found a niche market. We have the best programs available for serious minded statisticians doing academic or industrial computing. So any downturn in the economy doesn't hurt us as much as software companies, which concentrate on the home market. That, of course, doesn't mean we can letup. If we let down our guard, somebody else will move in and takeover our share of the market."

Steinberg and Ward said they planned to continue developing software for the use in the home.

"We know we're the under-dogs in the home financial market," Ward said. "Quicken and Microsoft products dominate the field. But other markets are wideopen and we aren't going to backdown just because we're the little guy."

Beside his responsibilities at Consolidated, Steinberg is President of the National Software Writers Association and lectures frequently at major Universities on the need for creativity in computer education. Ward is a trusty of Northern State University and on the board of directors of Jacksonville National Bank.

PART 2

Although these sentences have many kinds of errors, they emphasize who and whom.

1. Whoever wins in Georgia will probably defeat whoever wins in Iowa.
2. The man who killed the woman was identical to the man who police arrested.
3. The boy that was hit by the car will need x-rays.
4. Mickey Spillane, who wrote several books, is a man who police officers respect.
5. Writers who do not make much money often envy writers who make as much money as Spillane.
6. The athletes were told they could give their tickets to whoever wanted them.

CHAPTERS 3 AND 4
QUICK COURSE IN GRAMMAR AND PUNCTUATION

At some point in their college careers, many journalism majors discover that their knowledge of grammar isn't as sharp as they thought. They find themselves guessing whether a sentence needs a comma. Or worse, they've had grammatical errors in their work pointed out to them by editors during internships or by professors in writing and editing classes.

This crash course may help. We give you enough terminology for you to talk sensibly about grammar. Along the way, we tackle the most common grammar problems.

First we look at the parts of speech: nouns, pronouns, verbs, adjectives, adverbs, conjunctions and prepositions. Then we move on to phrases and clauses. You'll find a couple of exercises after each section. The answers to the first exercise in each section are in the back of the book.

We aren't going to claim that studying grammar is fun. We won't even claim it's the most important part of your journalism education. It is, however, the most fundamental. We contend that reporters who write grammatically correct stories have a better chance of keeping a job than reporters who don't. And we're sure you won't go far as a copy editor if you haven't mastered the basic rules of good grammar.

SECTION 1: NOUNS, PRONOUNS AND AGREEMENT

Nouns name people, places and things. The italicized words in the following sentences are nouns. Notice that a word can be a noun in one sentence and a modifier in another. For example, *computer* is a noun in the first sentence. In the second sentence, it modifies the noun *programs*.

> *Computers* have improved the *accuracy* of tax *forms* prepared by *individuals*, according to an IRS *representative*.
> Each *April*, *millions* of *Americans* buy computer *programs* to help them prepare their *taxes*.

Pronouns replace nouns. We usually think of pronouns as words such as *he, she, it, they, his, her, its* and so on. The noun that the pronoun replaces is called its antecedent. The pronouns are italicized in these sentences:

> The prosecutor told *him* that *his* client failed to answer *her* questions.
> The department assigned *its* best investigators to question *them* about *their* crimes.

Sometimes words such as *that, which, who* and *whom* can be pronouns, as in the following sentences:

> John Jones, *who* founded Express Airlines, was a pilot for Pan Am, *which* stopped flying in 1992.
> She worked for a company *that* manufactured explosives for the military.

Who, which and *that* take the place of the nouns *John Jones, Pan Am* and *company*. The writer did not have to repeat those words in the sentences.

Vague pronoun references can be confusing, as in this sentence:

> The university told the city it needed more police officers.

Does the pronoun *it* refer to city or to the university. Perhaps the university thinks the city is crime-ridden and needs more cops. Or does the pronoun *it* refer to *university*? The university is saying its own police department is too small. To clear up vague pronoun references, you can repeat the correct noun or recast the sentence:

Repeating noun: The university told the city that the university needed more police officers.
Recast: The city needs more police officers, a university representative said.
Recast: The university needs more police officers, a university representative told the City Council.

Two or more nouns can be the subject of a sentence. In those cases, we use plural verbs to agree with the subject. We say, "Jim and Betty are," not "Jim and Betty is." Here are more examples:

Not: The five Republicans and Johnson *has* objected.
But: The five Republicans and Johnson *have* objected.

Not: The five men and seven women of the jury *was* polled.
But: The five men and seven women of the jury *were* polled.

Collective nouns such as *jury, group, corporation, team* and *committee* are almost always singular in American English even though they represent lots of people: A jury may have six or 12 members, a football team usually has at least 50 players, and a corporation can have thousands of employees. Yet these words take singular verbs and pronouns, and that causes problems for some writers. Some advice: Almost no one has trouble using verbs correctly with collective nouns. Most of us say, "The team is on the field," not "The team are on the field." We recognize that *team* is singular, so we use the singular verb *is*. Similarly, we say, "The Chicago Bears are on the field," not "The Chicago Bears is on the field." We use the plural verb *are* with the plural noun *Bears*. The general rule: If you use singular verbs with a noun, you also need to use singular pronouns such as *it* and *its* to refer to the noun. If you use plural verbs, use plural pronouns such as *they* and *their*, as in these examples:

The jury announced *its* verdict.
The jurors announced *their* verdict.

Northern State University fired *its* coach despite having *its* first winning season in years.
The Northern State Blasters fired *their* coach despite having *their* first winning season in years.

A team of psychologists *is* expected to testify in his behalf.
Several psychologists *are* expected to testify in his behalf.

A group of students *was* arrested after the game.
Dozens of students *were* arrested after the game.

Occasionally you will run into sentences that sound more conversational if you use the plural version. Also, using the plural may allow you to avoid sexism. Each of the following sentences is grammatically correct. Depending on the facts and context, the second one in each pair may be a better choice:

The team refused to practice when *it* was told *it* would have to buy *its* own shoes this year.
The basketball players refused to practice when *they* were told *they* would have to buy *their* own shoes this year.

The jury told the judge *it* wanted to visit the scene.
Jurors told the judge *they* wanted to visit the scene.

Each student was told to submit *his* application by May 1.
Students were told to submit *their* applications by May 1.

Newspapers do not usually use the cumbersome "his or her" formulation.

Not: Each student must bring his or her camera.
But: Students must bring their cameras.

Some grammarians consider collective nouns plural if the members of the group are not working together. These grammarians may be correct about the grammar, but the end result often is a sentence that sounds odd. In those cases, it's better to look for another grammatically correct way to write the sentence.

Correct but awkward: The team are not in agreement on how to split the money. *Or* The team disagree on how to split the money.
Better: Team members are not in agreement on how to split the payoff. *Or* Team members disagree on how to split the payoff.

Each is singular. You say, "Each is," not "Each are." So use singular verbs and pronouns with the word *each*: "Each of them has asked for his money back." (If the sentence is discussing both men and women, you can use the plural form to avoid sexism: "All of them have asked for their money back.")

Each of the men *was* charged with burglary.
Each *was* released after posting bond.

Don't confuse these uses of *each* with its use in this sentence:

Not: The men each has requested public defenders.
But: The men each have requested public defenders.

In this sentence, *men* is the noun that serves as the subject of the verb. Because *men* is plural, the verb must also be plural (*have*).

Words between subjects and verbs usually make no difference in subject-verb agreement, except for a few special cases that we discuss shortly.

Not: Johnson, along with five Republicans, *have* objected.
But: Johnson, along with five Republicans, *has* objected.

Not: The jury of five men and seven women *were* polled.
But: The jury of five men and seven women *was* polled.

Not: The team of psychologists *have* examined the man.
But: The team of psychologists *has* examined the man.

Not: The discovery of three more victims *have* stunned police.
But: The discovery of three more victims *has* stunned police.

Not: Each of the students who won Stutzman Scholarships *have* done well in college.
But: Each of the students who won Stutzman Scholarships *has* done well in college.

Johnson, jury, discovery and *each* are singular, so the verbs must be singular: *has objected, was polled, has examined, has stunned* and *has done.*

Some exceptions to these guidelines are troublesome. Whether percentages and fractions are singular or plural depends on the words that follow them. If the word after *of* is plural, the verb is plural. If it's singular, the verb is singular. These sentences are correct:

Eight percent of the students *have* the flu.
Eight percent of the student body *has* the flu.
Eight percent *is* rather low for this time of year.

A quarter of the faculty *favors* the strike.
A quarter of the professors *favor* the strike.
A quarter is enough for now.

Number is singular when used with *the*, but plural with the article *a.*

A number of people have been killed by the storm.
The number of deaths has been difficult to determine.

Majority, plurality and **minority** can be singular or plural. When these words are used alone, they are singular:

The majority *has* decided not to announce *its* decision.
The left-wing minority *plans* to voice *its* opposition.

These words can be singular or plural when they are followed by a prepositional phrase, as in these examples:

A majority of the houses *were* destroyed by the storm.
A majority of the electorate *was* confused by the referendum.

Very rarely, you may run into this exception: When the word *majority* is the emphasis of the sentence, a singular verb is used.

A majority of two votes *is* needed.

EXERCISE 23   NAME _____

Practice exercise. Answers in back of book.

PART 1

In the following sentences, write N over the nouns and PRO over the pronouns.

1. Consolidated Computer Co. on Tuesday began to buy back computers with defective chips.

2. Customers who purchased computers with SV16 chips have four months to claim their refunds.

3. After Jackson was fired, he hacked his way into the company's computers and stole its secret formulas.

PART 2

Go through the sentences and pick the correct answer.

4. The airline industry, along with several large tourist agencies, (is, are) advertising lots of good deals.
5. Consolidated Airlines said Tuesday that (it, they) (was, were) cutting fares on (its, their) flights to London.
6. The number of people who bought the cheap tickets (was, were) higher than expected.
7. A number of customers (was, were) told that all the discounted seats had been sold.
8. A majority of them (was, were) very angry.
9. Every customer (was, were) offered a frequent-flier membership with 1,000 bonus miles.
10. About half of them (was, were) willing to accept the offer.
11. Consolidated said about 90 percent of the seats on Tuesday's flight (was, were) filled. Forty percent (is, are) considered good for this time of year, according to the airline.
12. Delta announced (it, they) would lower (its, their) prices, too.
13. American, along with Continental and Northwest, (has, have) already lowered (its, their) fares.
14. These airlines each (has, have) reported increased sales.
15. One travel agent said that 80 percent of his business (has, have) come from people seeking the low fares.
16. The board of trustees decided to postpone (its, their) meeting.
17. A jury of five men and seven women (was, were) selected to hear the rape case.
18. Jurors will be asked to hear all the evidence before (it reaches, they reach) a verdict.
19. The prosecution team told reporters later that (it, they) had wanted more women on the jury.
20. However, defense attorneys said that every accused man has a right to be tried by (his, their) peers.
21. A basketball team made up of retired professors (has, have) been asked to play a benefit game against members of the student senate.
22. During (its, their) road trip through the Midwest last year, the old-timers won most of (its, their) games.
23. A number of their opponents (was, were) embarrassed to lose to the older men.
24. The number of senior citizens involved in strenuous activity (has, have) climbed in recent years.
25. A number of doctors now (recommends, recommend) that older people participate in team sports.
26. However, each of the doctors (emphasize, emphasizes) that people should see (his or her, their) doctors before beginning strenuous exercise.
27. A 5-year-old boy along with his parents (was, were) killed in a fiery crash on Highway 31.
28. Neither the 5-year-old nor his parents (was, were) wearing seat belts.

29. Most people who died in accidents last year (was, were) not wearing them.
30. Forty percent of drivers (says, say) they think the belts are overly restrictive.
31. Eighty percent of the electorate (favors, favor) mandatory seat belt laws.
32. Rental companies say 90 percent of their customers (asks, ask) for four-door sedans.
33. Research says that an air bag combined with a seat belt (reduces, reduce) the likelihood the driver will be injured.
34. A baby seat, a cell phone and a full-size spare tire (is, are) standard equipment on all Save-a-Buck rental cars.
35. The League of Auto Users, a Chicago-based coalition of safety organizations, (believes, believe) more research should be done to make cars safer.

PART 3

These sentences may have agreement and hyphen problems. Fix them.

36. A team of officials from the Federal Aviation Administration and the Boeing Corporation are studying the airplane's flight recorders.

37. Shortly before the crash, the crew told air controllers that they were having trouble controlling the plane.

38. Boeing pledged to fix any problems found in airplanes they made.

39. On the team is Jorge Santana and Thurmond Maxwell.

40. After two rounds, the first place team are Betsy Tuggle and Paul Masson but Joyce Lacy and Roy Copeland are still the favored team.

41. Memphis will begin their season against a Knoxville team that already have won two games.

EXERCISE 24   NAME _____

PART 1

In the following sentences, write N over the nouns and PRO over the pronouns.

1. Police said the man fought them when they tried to handcuff him.

2. The man whom police arrested contends that intake officers at the jail broke his arm.

3. The man is suing the police department for $1 million.

4. He is a pianist who says his career has been ruined.

PART 2

Go through the sentences and pick the correct answer.

5. Consolidated Airlines has ordered 10 new jets, which will be used on (its, their) long-distance flights.
6. An airline official said Consolidated plans to use the new jets to double (its, their) flights between New York and Paris.
7. A number of airlines (has, have) purchased new jets for (its, their) fleets.
8. Northern State University's athletic department said Tuesday (it, they) will not allow (its, their) athletes to participate in a fund-raising event next week.
9. The group organizing the charity games (has, have) asked the university to reconsider (its, their) position.
10. The fund-raiser allows the department to buy many items (it, they) could not afford otherwise.
11. Each of the athletes (has, have) been told to stay away from the fund-raiser.
12. A university spokesman said a majority of the athletes (has, have) agreed not to play.
13. But a number of them (has, have) told organizers they will be there.
14. The president of the university, along with the leaders of the Faculty Senate, (thinks, think) the athletes should not participate.
15. A poll taken by the student newspaper found that more than half of the student body (thinks, think) the players should attend, and a third (sides, side) with the university. About 15 percent of the students (was, were) undecided.
16. A faculty committee announced (it, they) will look into charges of favoritism being shown athletes.
17. About 75 percent of the athletes (has, have) access to computers in their resident halls, but only 20 percent of the student body (lives, live) in dorms with computer facilities.
18. The Student Senate committee decided the students' private lives were none of (its, their) business.
19. A herd of cattle (is, are) blocking traffic on Interstate 40.
20. The cattle (was, were) aboard a truck that overturned.
21. A group of disgruntled employees (is, are) willing to expose the company's illegal practices.
22. The employees (has, have) hired an attorney.
23. A committee of reporters told the publisher that (it, they) believed the news hole was too small.
24. Eighty percent of the newspaper (is, are) filled with ads.
25. More than half the pages (has, have) nothing but ads.
26. The local paper and the chain that owns it (has, have) grown rapidly.
27. The student body will cast (its, their) votes Tuesday on a proposal to increase tuition.
28. The Cubs, playing without Clyde Overdorf, lost (its, their) first game of the season.

29. The number of small town newspapers (has, have) remained constant.
30. A number of afternoon dailies (has, have) closed in the past 10 years.
31. A number of newly elected politicians (favors, favor) term limits.
32. Only 10 percent of senior members of Congress (want, wants) term limits.
33. Either the president or the party regulars now (has, have) to rally support for the bill.
34. Ty Cobb, Babe Ruth and Mickey Mantle each (is, are) deserving of being in the Hall of Fame.
35. All of them (was, were) first rate baseball players.
36. Each of them (was, were) controversial in (his, their) own way.
37. If a British company treated (its, their) workers that poorly, (it, they) would face criminal charges.
38. General Motors, along with Ford and Honda, (has, have) asked the government to study the issue.
39. After receiving a standing ovation, the band played a rocking version of the university's fight song as (its, their) encore.

PART 3

Fix any errors in these sentences.

40. WNSU is the top-rated station just two months after they replaced their news anchors.

41. The new anchor team is Rock Phillips and Jane Paul. They are veteran reporters.

42. The weekend team of Coshi Ling and Evan Levine are also gaining viewership.

43. None of the reporters have more than two years experience. Each of them are lifelong residents of Northern City.

44. A number of stations from other markets is studying how WNSU improved their newscasts so quickly.

SECTION 2: MODIFIERS, PREPOSITIONS AND CONJUNCTIONS

Adjectives modify nouns. They change the reader's image of the nouns or give more information about them. The italicized words in these sentences are adjectives:

The *persistent* attorney demanded that the *industrial* complex not be located in the *quiet* neighborhood.
Computer programs make preparing *federal* taxes easier for the *average* citizen who files a *simple* return.

(Some people also call *the, a* and *an* adjectives; others label them *articles.*)

Adverbs modify verbs. Often they tell how, how often or when. They end in *-ly* so often that some people think of them as always ending in *-ly*. However, words such as *twice, never* and *often* can also be adverbs.

The coach *twice* signaled for a timeout.
The mayor whispered *softly* that she *never intentionally* misled the council.
The candidate *angrily* denied he was at the party and *then* accused his opponent of mudslinging.

Adverbs can also modify adjectives or other adverbs. The italicized words are adverbs in the following sentences:

The salesman was *overly* enthusiastic.
The witness said the car was *terribly* old and *very* dirty.
Police approached the bomb *very* carefully.

Remember that when adverbs modify adjectives and adverbs, you do not use hyphens.

Not: The highly-intelligent man made a completely-stupid comment.
But: The highly intelligent man made a completely stupid comment.

Prepositions such as *in, on, over, by* and *with* show how nouns are related to other words in the sentence. The preposition and the noun form a prepositional phrase. These sentences have several prepositions:

The body was found in the trunk of a car parked near the bridge on Main Street.
Students with tickets to the concert were excused from music classes in the afternoon.

In the trunk, of a car, near the bridge, on Main Street, with tickets, to the concert, from music classes and *in the afternoon* are prepositional phrases. *In, of, near, on, with, to, from* and *in* are prepositions in these sentences, and *trunk, car, bridge, Main Street, tickets, concert, classes* and *afternoon* are objects of the prepositions.

Note that prepositional phrases usually aren't set off by commas.

Not: Police found the drugs, in the trunk of the car.
But: Police found the drugs in the trunk of the car.

Not: A company, in Argentina, made the defective part.
But: A company in Argentina made the defective part.

Conjunctions connect ideas in sentences. The easy ones to spot are the coordinating conjunctions such as *and, or, either/or, neither/nor* and *but*. We talk about another kind of conjunction—subordinating conjunctions—when we discuss clauses.

Democrats lost the race for sheriff, *but* they won two seats on the County Council.
Italy *and* Spain plan to buy wheat from *either* Canada *or* the United States.

When either/or and neither/nor connect the subjects of a sentence, the noun closer to the verb determines whether the verb is singular or plural.

Neither the judge nor the attorneys *have* objected to the photographers.
Neither the attorneys nor the judge *has* objected to the photographers.

Either the team owners or the union *has* the right to demand a meeting.
Either the union or the team owners *have* the right to demand a meeting.

Use determines a word's part of speech. A word might be one part of speech in one sentence and another part of speech in another.

It's the best jail in the *county*. (noun)
Police took the man to the *county* jail. (adjective)

To can be used as a preposition, adverb or part of a verb form called an infinitive:

The boxer went *to* Iowa. (preposition)
He failed *to duck* when the champ threw a punch. (part of infinitive *to duck*)
A nurse was there when he came *to*. (adverb)

EXERCISE 25   NAME _____

Practice exercise. Answers in back of the book.

PART 1

Write ADV over any adverbs, ADJ over adjectives, PREP over prepositions, and OP over objects of prepositions.

1. For the first time in 50 years, angry customers can seek help from a government agency.

2. The law received overwhelming support from consumer groups.

3. The House passed the bill unanimously, but in the Senate it was debated bitterly.

4. The newly appointed attorney was angry when the judge quickly denied her request for a postponement.

5. The aging factories on the Ohio River belched sooty smoke.

PART 2

Fix the grammar and punctuation errors in the following sentences.

6. Stores, on Main Street, are quickly becoming profitable.

7. Neither the mayor nor the City Council have helped build trust.

8. The City Council should reconsider their plans for the area.

9. The merchants and the Chamber of Commerce is planning a celebration.

10. Either the police officers or the mayor are lying.

11. The fire, at the Reilly Box Company, burned for hours.

12. Neither the incumbent nor his challengers were willing to debate.

13. Police seized the newly-painted car.

EXERCISE 26   NAME _____

PART 1

Write ADV over any adverbs, ADJ over adjectives, PREP over prepositions, and OP over objects of prepositions.

1. Nine people matched the winning numbers in this week's lottery.

2. They will split the largest prize in the brief history of the lottery.

3. Police said the psychotic gunmen fought furiously until they doused him with tear gas.

4. The newly elected mayor fought bitterly with the outgoing director of public utilities.

5. Politicians in small towns often battle continuously over totally insignificant issues.

6. Before the attack, he ran the most successful espresso stand in lower Manhattan.

PART 2

Fix the grammar and punctuation errors in the following sentences.

7. Jackson's father died in the war, against Germany.

8. Neither the Veterans Association nor the Army plan to help make the movie.

9. The association has a clause in their bylaws prohibiting them from participating in movies.

10. The location and the subject matter is still too painful, to many people.

11. Neither the filmmakers nor the public are likely to compromise on the script.

12. The recently-revised script dropped many of the most objectionable words.

13. Some objected to the hastily-written changes because they said they made the script "sickeningly-sweet."

SECTION 3: SUBJECTS, OBJECTS AND VERBS

Active verbs are the mainstays of journalistic writing. Most sentences follow the subject-verb-object order. They tell who or what did something, what was done, and to whom or to what it was done. Those kinds of sentences demand active verbs. Take these sentences:

The mayor sued the paper.
The president has the flu.

In the first sentence, *mayor* is the subject (she's doing the suing), *sued* is the active verb, and *paper* is the direct object (it's receiving the action). In the second, *president* is the subject, *has* is the active verb, and *flu* is the direct object. Not all active verbs have direct objects. Active verbs that have direct objects are called *transitive verbs;* those that don't have direct objects are *intransitive*. Here are sentences with active verbs that do not have direct objects:

The trucker drove through the night.
The car slammed into a brick wall.

Drove and *slammed* are active verbs, but the sentences do not have direct objects. *Night* and *wall* are objects of the prepositions, not direct objects.

With passive verbs, the subject is receiving the action, as in this sentence:

The paper was sued by the mayor.

Was sued is a passive verb. *Paper* is the subject of the sentence even though it is receiving the action. Notice that passive verbs do not have direct objects. (*Mayor* is the object of the preposition *by*.) Here are some guidelines for telling passive-voice verbs from active-voice ones:

- With active verbs, subjects of sentences are doing the activity.
- With passive verbs, subjects of sentences receive the action.
- Passive verbs never have direct objects; active verbs often do.

These sentences have active verbs:

Brown *hit* a home run in the sixth inning.
Vandals *damaged* eight police cars Tuesday night.
An assassin *killed* President Kennedy in Dallas in 1963.
A Coast Guard ship *found* a fully armed torpedo from World War II floating in Puget Sound on Tuesday.

Here are similar sentences written to have passive verbs:

A home run *was hit* by Brown in the sixth inning.
Eight police cars *were vandalized* Tuesday night.
President Kennedy *was assassinated* in Dallas in 1963.
A fully armed torpedo from World War II *was found* floating in Puget Sound on Tuesday by a Coast Guard ship.

Editors prefer active verbs. They give sentences energy and make stories more readable. Whenever you see a passive verb, ask yourself whether you can make the sentence stronger by using an active verb. However, don't assume that passive voice is always bad. Sometimes passive verbs allow writers to emphasize the who or what of a story. Many editors probably would leave alone these passive-voice sentences:

The Empire State Building, one of the world's first skyscrapers, will be torn down next year to make room for a parking garage.

A deadly coral snake was found in a package mailed to a doctor at the Colonial Street Women's Clinic on Monday, according to police.

Linking verbs equate things. Because they don't show action, it doesn't make much sense to talk about their subjects as doing anything or their objects as receiving that action. With linking verbs, the noun before the verb is considered the subject and the noun after the verb is a predicate noun or predicate nominative. Here are two sentences:

John Matthews is the editor of the paper.
The editor of the paper is John Matthews.

In the first sentence, *John Matthews* is the subject, and *editor* is a predicate noun. In the second sentence, *editor* is the subject, and *John Matthews* becomes the predicate noun. If the subject is singular, the verb must be singular. If the subject is plural, the verb is plural, too. So:

The new anchor team *is* Paul Brown and Dorothy Pitts.
Paul Brown and Dorothy Pitts *are* the new anchor team.

Linking verbs can also be followed by adjectives that modify the subject, as do *old* and *well-worn* in the next example. The *AP Stylebook* calls for hyphens in compound modifiers even when they are predicate adjectives coming after forms of the verb *to be*.

His dictionary was old and well-worn.

Don't confuse linking verbs with helping verbs. In the following sentences, *is, has* and *were* are not linking verbs. They are part of the verbs *is reading, was passed, were arrested* and *were seen*.

The president *is reading* a bill that *was passed* by Congress.
Two men *were arrested* after they *were seen* running from the bank.

Infinitives are verb forms that start with *to*: to raid, to consider, to think, to be. (*To be* is the infinitive form of *is, was, were* and so on.)

The police wanted *to raid* the fraternity and *search* for the missing kegs of beer. (The *to* before search is understood.)
The retired principal said he wouldn't want *to be* a teacher in today's schools.
To be seen at the Cannes Film Festival is important if she is *to get* the attention she needs.

Lie and lay are easy to use correctly if you remember what they mean. *Lie* means to rest, to do nothing. *Lay* means to place, to put something somewhere. It involves an action. These sentences are correct:

Some older people lie in bed all day. *(rest, do nothing)*
But Jenkins still lays bricks every day with his son. *(places bricks)*
The book lies on the table. *(rests, does nothing)*
He will lay the book on the table. *(place the book)*

Lie/lay become trickier in the past tense.

Present tense	Past tense
Lie	lay
Lay	laid

Some examples:

He lay dead in the street for hours before he was discovered.
She laid out her plans for the department at yesterday's meeting.

The *–ing* forms of these verbs are *lying* and *laying.*

He was lying in the gutter when he was found.
The company is laying off workers.

EXERCISE 27   NAME _____

Practice exercise. Answers in back of book.

PART 1

In the following sentences, write S over subjects, AV over active verbs, PV over passive verbs and LV over linking verbs.

1. The council approved funding for road improvements but rejected plans for a bike path.

2. Most of the improvements will be to roads around Quality Fair Shopping Mall.

3. The new roads will allow easy access to the mall from Route 50.

4. Without the road improvements, the planning board would not approve the expansion.

5. The mall is the largest shopping facility in the county.

6. Mayor Roberta Simms campaigned against the expansion but then voted for it.

7. Simms was widely criticized by voters who thought she had betrayed them.

8. Honesty in government was a theme in her campaign.

9. Traffic around the mall has grown dramatically in the past 10 years.

10. The expansion will make a bad situation even worse, according to many residents.

11. The decision was based on a 3-year-old report, the residents said.

12. Four new lanes will be added to Georgia Street between Kings Avenue and 39th Street.

13. Fifteen years ago the area was a peaceful valley with few homes and quaint shops.

14. Mall owners' plans include a new department store, specialty shops and a food court.

15. Many shoppers hope that the new stores will offer more selection and that the added competition will

    bring prices down.

PART 2

Rewrite the following sentences, turning any passive verbs into active ones.

16. Dinosaur bones were discovered on the banks of White River by two hunters.

17. Northern State University President Richard Aster was charged Tuesday with first-degree murder in

    the death of the president of the NSU faculty senate.

18. Mississippi beaches were battered for a second straight day Tuesday as Hurricane Lola continued to stir up the Gulf of Mexico.

19. A law has been passed by the City Council that will prohibit the overnight parking of large trucks and recreational vehicles on city streets.

20. Tuesday's concert was canceled after a bomb threat was received by organizers.

PART 3

Use lie/lay correctly.

21. Jimenez refused to (lie, lay) off the workers.
22. Jimenez refused to (lie, lay) on the sofa.
23. The robber ordered the customers to (lie, lay) on the floor.
24. The police officer ordered the robber to (lie, lay) his gun on the floor.
25. Johns (laid, lay) in the morgue until a worker noticed he was breathing.
26. The most important clue (laid, lay) on top of the desk in plain view
27. The gambler (laid, lay) his cards on the table and claimed his prize.

EXERCISE 28   NAME _____

PART 1

In the following sentences, write S over subjects and an AV over active verbs; LV over linking verbs and a PV over passive verbs.

1. The Panthers are the best team in the conference, according to a poll of sportswriters.

2. The Panthers have three of the best linemen in the country.

3. They have won at least nine games each season for 10 years in a row.

4. Although they lost quarterback Steve Rodgers for the season when he broke his leg, the Panthers have two freshmen who would be starters at most schools.

5. Rodgers broke his leg when he slipped off a bar stool.

6. Four fractures were found when his leg was X-rayed.

7. Bob Smith was sentenced to 20 years in prison even though his wife was given 120 days in the county jail for the same crime.

8. The governor was not present when the crime was committed.

9. Northern State University on Tuesday announced plans for four new residence halls, which will be built in the next three years.

10. Bernie McDermitt, who claimed he was kidnapped by a female motorcycle gang, admitted today that he made up the story so that he could be on a TV talk show.

PART 2

Rewrite these sentences to get rid of any passive verbs.

11. Five bridges were destroyed Tuesday by a storm that ripped through the county.
12. Flood waters blocked most major highways and brought traffic to a halt.
13. Five men were arrested outside the arena and charged with selling unlicensed T-shirts.
14. Police said a professor on his way to a 7 a.m. class was robbed Tuesday.
15. The man said he was beaten by police officers with clubs.
16. A parked car was rammed by a wayward moose.
17. Topless clubs must be relocated to areas of the city that have been zoned for industrial use, according to a law passed by the City Council Tuesday night.
18. Alcoholic beverages will no longer be served at fraternity parties, the dean said.
19. A starter on Northern State's basketball team was indicted Tuesday by a grand jury on charges of fixing games last season.

20. His leg had to be amputated to stop the spread of the disease, according to doctors.
21. Identification cards with smart chips will be given to students.
22. The cards will allow students to check out books from the library, charge purchases at all on-campus and many off-campus businesses and use computers in the university's computer labs.
23. Credit limits have been set at $500.
24. Students who used the cards on a trial basis were enthusiastic about them.

PART 3

Use lie and lay correctly.

25. The body (lies, lays) in the street while the detective questions the suspect.
26. The body was still (lying, laying) in the street several hours later.
27. The book (lay, laid) on a shelf in the library for 50 years.
28. The president (lay, laid) out his plans for tax reform.
29. The caddie was fired after he (lay, laid) the score card on the wrong table.
30. After (lying, laying) claim to America, Columbus became a hero in Spain.

SECTION 4: COMMAS, CLAUSES AND PHRASES

Groups of words with subjects and verbs are called clauses; word groupings without subjects and verbs are phrases. "He won the race" and "after she was re-elected" are clauses. They have subjects and verbs. "In the last quarter" and "after running the race" are phrases.

Independent clauses express complete thoughts and therefore can be complete sentences:

The mayor sued the paper.

Mayor is the subject of the clause; *sued* is the verb. Independent clauses can have more than one subject:

The mayor and the City Council sued the paper.

Both mayor and council are subjects of the clause, and sued is the verb. Independent clauses can also have more than one verb:

The mayor read the story and then decided to sue the paper.

Mayor is the subject of the sentence. The verbs are *read* and *decided*. The mayor did both of those actions. There's no comma before *and* because mayor is the subject of both verbs.

When two or more independent clauses are in the same sentence, some writers have trouble with the punctuation. For example, "Northern State's Blasters are ranked 20th in the nation by the AP this week" is an independent clause. "NSU's Moe Collins was named coach of the week by *USA Today*" is also an independent clause. If we combine them in one sentence, we get:

Northern State's Blasters are ranked 20th in the nation by the AP this week, and NSU's Moe Collins was named coach of the week by *USA Today*.

Notice that when we combine two long independent clauses, we must put a comma before the conjunction. If we combine the two clauses without a conjunction such as "and" or "but," we need to use a semicolon instead of a comma:

Northern State had its best season in years; Southern State lost every game.

A semicolon is also used when two independent clauses are connected with a conjunctive adverb, such as *however*. Notice that a comma goes after *however*:

Northern State had its best season in years; however, many alumni wanted to fire Coach Moe Collins.

More commonly, journalists use two sentences:

Northern State had its best season in years. However, many alumni wanted to fire Coach Moe Collins.

Dependent clauses are groups of words that have subjects and verbs but don't seem to be complete thoughts. For example, "After the mayor read the story" is a clause. It has a subject (*mayor*) and a verb (*read*), but it's not a complete thought. It depends on another clause to make sense. If we add a dependent clause to an independent clause, we get perfectly fine sentences:

> After the mayor read the story, she sued the paper.
> The mayor sued the paper after she read the story.

Dependent clauses often begin with subordinating conjunctions such as *after, before, while,* or with relative pronouns such as *that, who, whom, which.* In the following examples, the dependent clauses are in italics.

> *While she was running for mayor,* Simms discovered she had skin cancer.
> He was a has-been *before he got to enjoy his stardom.*
> The restaurant *that the health department closed last month* has filed for bankruptcy.
> Ma's Supper Bar, *which the health department closed last month,* has filed for bankruptcy.

Prepositional phrases, discussed previously, are rarely set off by commas.

> *Not:* Johnson entered the Democratic primary, in 1964.
> *But:* Johnson entered the Democratic primary in 1964.

However, when attribution is provided using a prepositional phrase beginning with *according to,* the phrase is normally set off. Also, long prepositional phrases at the beginning of sentences may be set off.

> *Not:* Branson was never charged with a crime according to court records.
> *But:* Branson was never charged with a crime, according to court records.

> *Not:* In the year after the World War II started building ships became a national priority.
> *But:* In the year after the World War II started, building ships became a national priority.

Participle phrases begin with a verb form called a *participle.* Participles often end in *-ing.* However, because they are verbs, they can also be in the past tense and end in *-ed* or other letters. Here are some sentences with participle phrases. When participle phrases are at the beginning of a sentence, they are usually set off by commas. In the following sentences, *needing, wanted* and *sensing* are participles. The participle phrases are in italics:

> *Needing to graduate in the fall,* he attended summer school.
> *Wanted by the FBI,* he tried to obtain a phony passport.
> The attorney, *sensing her client was nervous,* asked for a recess.

When phrases are the subject of the sentence, do not put a comma after them.

> *Not:* Losing the Indiana primary, was a major setback.
> *But:* Losing the Indiana primary was a major setback.

EXERCISE 29 NAME _____

Practice exercise. Answers in back of book.

PART 1

Correct the punctuation in these sentences.

1. Before McCoy discovered the joys of journalism she was a chemistry major.

2. Although the Yankees won the pennant the team's owner fired the manager and criticized the team's dedication.

3. Angry fans threw coins at the referees and officials cleared the arena and gave the victory to the Wildcats.

4. The prosecutor pointed his finger and called the youths "murderous misfits."

5. After pointing his finger at the youths the prosecutor called them "murderous misfits."

6. After the prosecutor pointed his finger at the youths he called them "murderous misfits."

7. The Cubs will play the Braves on Tuesday at Wrigley Field but the White Sox have the day off to recover after losing Monday's doubleheader.

8. Bob Smith was convicted of bank robbery but found not guilty of the murder of the guard according to court records.

9. Police said the governor was not present when the crime occurred.

10. General Motors increased the prices on its cars but Ford and Chrysler announced price cuts.

11. An AP reporter was told about the senator's decision and quickly filed her story.

12. An AP reporter was told about the senator's decision but her editors decided the story was too speculative and refused to use it.

13. Reporters lose their tempers when editors make such decisions.

14. The reporter threatened to sue the editors, however no one thought she was serious.

15. The boy was found, in Dallas, with four other runaways.

16. Running a major corporation, Tidler had little time for his family.

17. Running a major corporation often strains relationships.

PART 2

In the following sentences, write S over subjects, P over participles and V over verbs. Correct any punctuation problems.

18. The company will buy traffic lights for the intersection and the city will pay to widen the road.

19. After having breakfast with Baptist ministers, the governor spoke to supporters at a Unitarian church.

20. Suffering from a severe case of tennis elbow, Myers withdrew from a tournament in Rome but she said she will play in the French Open next month.

EXERCISE 30   NAME _____

PART 1

In the following sentences, write an S over the subjects, P over participles and V over verbs.

1. The bank president was arrested after the money was found in his gym locker.

2. After talking to an accountant, Miller sold his home in Texas before the tax deadline.

3. Although most small newspapers pay low salaries, they give lots of experience to beginning reporters.

4. The company knew it was in trouble when reporters from "60 Minutes" asked for interviews.

5. Wheat prices hit record highs after the drought destroyed most of the crop in Kansas.

6. Raging unnoticed for two hours, a fire destroyed the oldest building in Andersonville Tuesday.

PART 2

Punctuate these sentences correctly.

7. Stock prices hit a record high Tuesday on the New York Stock Exchange but bond prices fell to an all-time low.

8. Stock prices were much higher Tuesday in Japan but fell 30 points in London.

9. The Dow Jones average held steady Thursday and many experts predicted that the rally was over.

10. Police raided four massage parlors on International Drive on Tuesday and arrested eight women on charges of public lewdness.

11. Police also arrested five male customers inside the massage parlors however prosecutors said it was unlikely they would be charged.

12. Hoping to rally support in Indiana Mercer visited the Indianapolis Motor Speedway.

13. The Raiders pledged to win the Super Bowl, the Giants said no way.

14. The knife fight was over before the children arrived according to police.

15. In the years before the company's collapse Jackson embezzled several million dollars government records charge.

SECTION 5: MORE COMMAS, CLAUSES AND PHRASES

Just as individual words serve as subjects, objects and modifiers, phrases and dependent clauses also can be subjects, objects and modifiers.

Modifying phrases and clauses are in italics in these sentences:

Consolidated Airlines, *which filed for bankruptcy last week,* laid off 300 employees Tuesday.
Determined to make the team, she worked out with weights all summer.

The clause *which filed for bankruptcy last week* modifies Consolidated Airlines. The clause changes our image of the company. The phrase *determined to make the team* modifies the pronoun *she*.

Noun phrases and clauses can be subjects of sentences. In the following sentences, the subject of the verb *haunted* is the clause *That he was defeated by only five votes.* The phrase *Winning the war* is the subject of the second sentence.

That he was defeated by only five votes haunted Miller for the rest of his political career.
Winning the war was the only thing on his mind.

Notice that when the noun phrase or clause is subject of the sentence, there are no commas between it and verb.

Not: Knowing he had done the right thing, made him happy.
But: Knowing he had done the right thing made him happy.

Not: That he was named coach of the year, was small consolation to Collins.
But: That he was named coach of the year was small consolation to Collins.

Clauses can also be direct objects. There are no commas between noun clauses and verbs:

Not: MacNeil sensed, *that his political career was over.*
But: MacNeil sensed *that his political career was over.*

Not: The coach predicted, the Tigers will win by at least 12 points.
But: The coach predicted the Tigers will win by at least 12 points.

Not: The president said, he did not want to raise fees.
But: The president said he did not want to raise fees.

However, commas are used with direct quotations when they are complete sentences.

The coach said, "We will win by at least 12 points."
The president said, "I do not want to raise fees."

Commas are usually not used with partial quotes.

Not: The president said he would, "never ever raise fees."
But: The president said he would "never ever raise fees."

Not: The company promised, "a completely emission-free car that is safe and comfortable."
But: The company promised "a completely emission-free car that is safe and comfortable."

Just as an individual word can be a noun in one sentence and a verb or a modifier in another, a clause or a phrase can be a modifier in some sentences and a subject or object in others:

Modifier: Hoping to win the sympathy of the jurors, the attorney had his client dress in somber clothing.
Subject: Hoping to win the sympathy of the jurors is a popular trick among many defense attorneys.

Introductory modifying phrases and clauses are almost always set off by commas unless they are very short. The introductory phrases and clauses are in italics in these examples:

Riding his bike from Orlando to New Orleans, the middle-aged man discovered an inner strength.
After his daughter was charged with shoplifting, he hired the best attorneys in town.
In front of 50,000 screaming fans in Wegner Stadium, the Tigers suffered their first loss in two years.
In 1994 the mayor won re-election.

Remember that we are talking about introductory phrases and clauses. When the same phrases and clauses are at the ends of sentences, they often do not have commas. Here are some examples:

Before the mayor vetoed the bill, she checked with the city attorney.
The mayor checked with the city attorney *before she vetoed the bill.*

While he was in Africa, he learned of several natural medicines.
He learned of several natural medicines *while he was in Africa.*

On the advice of his attorneys, Cooper refused to answer the question.
Cooper refused to answer the question *on the advice of his attorneys.*

EXERCISE 31   NAME _____

Practice exercise. Answers in back of book.

Add commas to these sentences, and correct other style and grammar problems you encounter.

1. The president of Consolidated Airlines said the company was losing money.

2. After Consolidated Airline's stock dropped more than 40 points in a single day many investors decided to sell all their stock in transportation companies.

3. Seeing Consolidated Airline's stock drop more than 40 points in a single day caused many investors to sell all their holdings in transportation companies.

4. Giving smokeless tobacco to children under 16 will be against the law if the bill passes.

5. Flying through a thunderstorm the plane was struck by lightning.

6. The plane was not damaged even though it was struck by lightning.

7. After Tompkins finished writing a biography of Truman she began a mystery novel.

8. Tompkins finished writing a biography of Truman and then began work on a novel.

9. Tompkins had just finished writing a biography of Truman when she began work on a novel.

10. After speaking with his client the lawyer accepted the plea bargain.

11. He told the prosecutor that his client had information about the mob.

12. He said "my client can spill the beans on more bad guys than you know about."

13. Although union leaders say they want an early settlement they will not accept pay cuts of any kind.

14. One union leader said company officials were "fat cats of the worse kind."

15. After dropping the fly in the fifth inning Smith hammered a home run in the eighth.

EXERCISE 32   NAME _____

Add commas to these sentences, and correct other style and grammar problems you encounter.

1. The company said it is losing money but union representatives say it is highly profitable.

2. Demanding that pilots accept pay cuts Sandra Means president of Air South threatened to fire all their pilots and begin looking for replacements.

3. Before becoming president of the airline Means was a professor at the Yale Law School and worked as an attorney in the Labor Department under President George Bush.

4. Means said she would resign before she would let a union dictate wages to her.

5. Much of the South is reeling from a monthlong draught but the Midwest is soggy after four days of steady downpours.

6. Before buying the house Langford checked mortgage rates at his local bank and asked the police about the crime rate in the neighborhood.

7. Stealing cash donations from collection boxes in malls Simpson pocketed more than $100,000 during his first year as chairman of the Brinkley Society.

8. Stealing cash donations from a charity is easy to do according to accountants.

9. Although charity leaders hate bad publicity of any kind they decided to press charges against Simpson.

10. One charity official said Simpson was "the evilest man I ever met."

11. After denying the charges for months Simpson finally admitted he took the money.

12. The university offered the professor his choice of receiving a $1 million settlement or being given tenure in the physics department.

SECTION 6: COMMAS AND NONESSENTIAL INFORMATION

No commas are used with essential clauses and phrases. They give information that is essential in identifying the nouns they modify, as in this example:

Students who have not paid their fees will be expelled.

Of all the students on campus, who will be expelled? Only the ones who have not paid their fees. The clause *who have not paid their fees* is essential. Another example:

The company that made the game has been sued for $10 million.

There are lots of companies. Which one has been sued for $10 million? The one that made the game. The clause *that made the game* is considered essential because it narrows our understanding of which company has been sued. Phrases can also be essential, as in this sentence:

He said he puts his money in the bank offering the best deal.

The phrase *offering the best deal* helps identify the kind of bank the man will use.

Nonessential clauses and phrases are set off by commas. These clauses and phrases provide interesting—even highly relevant—information, but the information is not essential to helping us understand who or what is being written about, as in the following sentences:

Consolidated Toy Company, which made the game, has been sued for $10 million.
Courtney Black, who has not paid her tuition, may be expelled.
He decided to put his money in Merchants National Bank, which offered him the best deal.

Appositives can also be essential or nonessential. Appositives are words or phrases that come after nouns. They are set off by commas when they are nonessential. They are not set off by commas when they are essential, as in these examples.

Essential appositive: Woody Allen's movie "Sleeper" is studied in film classes.
Nonessential appositive: Jackson, an attorney from Chicago, will represent him.

Allen made many movies. The appositive *Sleeper* is essential to identifying which movie is being studied. In the second sentence, the name *Jackson* identifies the man. The appositive *an attorney from Chicago* gives interesting information, but it is not essential to identifying him. Two more examples:

Bender's mother, Gladys Knight, attended the ceremony.
Bender's son John said he liked growing up in a large family with six brothers.

Bender has only one mother. Her name isn't needed to identify her. But because Bender has several sons, the name is essential to identifying which son is being quoted.

That and which. Nonessential clauses that modify things usually begin with *which*. They never begin with *that*. Essential clauses almost always begin with *that*. (They can start with *which* if the word *that* has already appeared in the passage several times.) Here are some examples:

Essential: The company *that invents a pocket-sized computer* will make lots of money.
Nonessential: Acme Computer Corp., *which invented a pocket-sized computer,* made lots of money.

When clauses modify people, they begin with *who* or *whom*, never *that* or *which*. Use commas with nonessential clauses.

Not: Any driver *that refuses to wear seat belts* should be fined.
But: Any driver *who refuses to wear seat belts* should be fined.

Essential: Any boxer *who can knock out Duke Jones* should be considered a contender.
Nonessential: Sly Dixon, *who knocked out Duke Jones,* should be considered a contender.

The choice of who and whom is made easier now that you understand clauses and phrases. *Who* is used for subjects of clauses and *whom* is used for objects. The first step is to isolate the clause or phrase. Look at these three sentences:

He sold drugs to whoever had the money.
He sold the drugs to whom?
To whom did he sell the drugs?

In the first sentence, the *who/whom* choice is in the clause *whoever had the money.* Because the *who/whom* choice is the subject of the clause, *whoever* is correct. Don't let the preposition *to* confuse you. The whole clause is the object of the preposition *to.* In the second and third sentences, we use *whom* because it is the object of the preposition *to.* Read this pair of sentences:

The attorney works hard for whoever pays him.
The attorney works hard for whomever he represents.

In the first sentence, the *whoever/whomever* choice is the subject of the verb *pays* in the clause *whoever pays him.* In the second sentence, *whomever* is direct object of the verb *represents.* In normal word order, the clause would read: *he represents whomever.* In both sentences, the clauses are the objects of the preposition *for.*

Confused by subjects and objects? A simple substitution may help. Substitute *he* for *who* and *him* for *whom.* Select the one that sounds right.

The candidate *who/whom* wins in Iowa is likely to be elected president.

Substituting *he* and *him* for *who* or *whom*, we get either *he wins in Iowa* or *him wins in Iowa.* He sounds better, so the correct choice is *who.* You still have to put the words in the normal word order.

The ACLU said it would represent whoever/whomever police arrested.

The *whoever/whomever* choice is in the clause *whoever/whomever police arrested.* Put the clause in normal word order: *police arrested whoever/whomever.* Substitute *he* and *him. Police arrested him* sounds better than *police arrested he.* The correct choice is *whomever.*

EXERCISE 33   NAME _____

Practice exercise. Answers in back of book.

Add commas to these sentences, and correct other style and grammar problems you encounter.

1. Fifteen students who were arrested at Saturday's game were expelled today by Provost Marcella Jones who said she was ashamed of the students' conduct.

2. Professor Claude Wilkens who admitted he took bribes from students was fired.

3. People who hope to make a living writing must be versatile.

4. Families that lost children in Tuesday's crash have sued the Acme Bus Company which leased the bus to the church.

5. Northern Brewery Inc. is expected to buy Southern Beer who recently fired their CEO.

6. Professors who will get pay raises under the new agreement, praised union leaders.

7. Tompkins who finished writing a biography of Truman last week is now working on a novel.

8. Married students who live on campus pay more for housing than single students do.

9. Bette Xavier who lives in Clarke Hall said she may sue the university unless they change the policy.

10. Police said the woman that robbed the 7-11 on Main Street used a toy pistol.

11. Police said they have no information about who robbed the bank.

12. The World Cup that is played every four years showcases the world's best soccer players.

13. Students who saw the incident disagreed with Sheriff Bill Bianchi who said the shooting was justified.

14. Maurice Daniels who won the lottery said he will quit his part time job.

15. Microsoft that makes the Windows operating system said they will sue any company who violates their copyrights.

16. A journalism professor who promised his classes he would not assign homework was named teacher of the year by the student body.

EXERCISE 34   NAME _____

PART 1

   Add commas to these sentences. Make sure which, that and who are used correctly. Correct any style or grammar problems.

   1. Fewer students will attend football games if the university doubles the price of tickets.

   2. Students who learn foreign languages have more chances of getting jobs abroad.

   3. Megan Wilson who speaks three languages wants to work in the AP's Paris bureau.

   4. After finding the child's body the firefighter leaned against his truck and wept uncontrollably.

   5. Sen. Darrell Kingston who was convicted last year on charges of abusing a teen-age aid refused to answer questions from leaders of the National Organization for Women that has called for his resignation.

   6. Buying a new car from a dealer should not be an ordeal.

   7. Any politician who promises to lower taxes and balance the budget is likely to win the editorial support of the Daily Bulletin-Telegram and its editor Clem Willard.

   8. University Health Service which in the past has provided free flu shots to students will begin charging $10 for the shots this fall.

   9. The mayor planned to buy police cars from any dealership that offered the city a good deal.

  10. The mayor decided to buy police cars from Andersonville Ford that offered the city a good deal.

  11. A student that ran onto the field and slugged a referee was taken to Lakeview Hospital's mental ward for observation.

  12. University President Robert Aster planned to use student fees to repair the president's mansion on campus but the NSU student senate that normally rubber-stamps the president's requests voted unanimously to spend the money in other ways.

  13. Lt. Paul Jackson who was in charge of security at the concert told police dispatchers that he shot a gang member that pulled a knife on him.

14. Andersonville City Council members that voted last week to fire the police chief changed their minds at last night's meeting.

15. Any journalism program which requires students to study computer-aided reporting will need first-rate computer facilities.

16. Northern State's journalism program that requires students to study computer-aided reporting needed to upgrade its computer facilities.

17. After reading the report NSU President Richard Aster approved the purchase of 30 new computers for the university's journalism department that had not upgraded their labs in 11 years.

18. New computers will allow the department to offer advanced graphics courses but some professors believe the students need more instruction in grammar.

19. Consolidated Computers which submitted the low bid is owned by Rahed Mohammed who graduated from NSU with a degree in journalism.

20. His bid was for $60,000 less than the one submitted by Ace Business Machines.

21. The computers will be installed in a graphics lab in the Booker Journalism Building this summer and will be ready when classes begin in the fall.

22. The man who stole the painting must have known something about the work of Charles White who was one of the 19th century's top artists.

23. The Indiana Pacers who play the Boston Celtics on Tuesday have offered the Celtics $10 million for the rights to Henry Williams whom many consider the NBA's best player.

24. Senior citizens who attended the opening celebration for the civic center said it was too small.

25. Many political insiders say that any candidate who promises to lower taxes will defeat Gov. Martha Wilson who said she intends to raise them.

26. The driver that wins the most NASCAR races during the winter months rarely wins any races during the long hot summers.

27. Drivers who refuse to wear seat belts, should be required to pay higher insurance premiums.

28. Richard Petty who won the Daytona 500 and several other NASCAR events never won the Indianapolis 500 which is probably the most famous race in the world.

29. Faulkner's first novel *Soldier's Pay* is often considered one of the worst novels by a major American writer but many consider his novel *The Sound and the Fury* one of the 20th century's best.

30. Johnson won his first case in Jacksonville Iowa in August 1985 and was appointed a federal judge in Jackson Mississippi on March 10 1998 by President George Bush.

SECTION 7: HYPHENS, MODIFIERS AND VERBS

Hyphens are not used with *-ly* **adverbs.** There are no hyphens between adverbs that end in *-ly* and the adjectives they modify. That's true even when the adverb ending in *-ly* and the adjective come before the noun.

Not: The newly-elected mayor said her party would have an easy time revising the city's severely-outdated codes.
But: The newly elected mayor said her party would have an easy time revising the city's severely outdated codes.

Hyphens are used with other adverbs. When adverbs that do not end in *-ly* modify adjectives in front of nouns, you usually need hyphens. (The adverb *very* is an exception to this rule.)

The well-known author signed autographs.
A better-qualified applicant could not be found.
The very angry man was dragged from the meeting.

Word groupings such as *hold up, tie down* **and** *lay off* are not hyphenated when they are used as verbs. However, when they're used as nouns and adjectives, some of these word groupings are hyphenated and some are not. You'll probably need to look them up. Try the *AP Stylebook* first and then go to *Webster's New World Dictionary*. Here are two examples:

The *holdup* men struck again. They tried to *hold up* the First Union bank.
The traffic *tie-up* was caused by a farmer who stopped to *tie up* a goat he was hauling.

Hyphens with compound modifiers. When you have two words that work together to modify a noun, they often form a compound modifier and are hyphenated. For example, in "the front-page story," the words *front* and *page* work together to modify *story*. The writer does not mean it's a "front story" and a "page story." Here are more examples:

A silver-haired bandit has committed several late-night robberies at 24-hour groceries.
She took a full-time job with a small-town newspaper.
The 3-year-old company reported third-quarter profits.

Use hyphens only when these words are compound adjectives in front of nouns. They're not hyphenated in other usages. Here are sentences similar to the ones above, but we've rewritten them so that they do not have compound adjectives:

A bandit with silver hair specializes in robberies late at night at groceries that are open 24 hours a day.
She works full time for a newspaper in a small town.
The company is 3 years old and reported profits for the third quarter.

When two equal adjectives are in front of a noun, you often use commas, not hyphens. Unlike compound modifiers, equal adjectives modify the noun independently. For example, "small, cluttered office" means it is a small office and a cluttered office. Here are some sentences with equal adjectives.

The long, hot summer faded into a damp, dreary fall.
He piled his old, worn-out clothes into his green station wagon.

There's no comma between *green* and *station* because station is part of the name of the vehicle. A rule of thumb: If you can substitute "and," you probably need the comma. Because you could say "a long and hot summer," you have the comma. However, "a green and station wagon" doesn't sound right. So there's no comma.

Prepositions or adverbs? Remember that words such as *in, to, up,* and *down* are not always prepositions. Often we use them much like adverbs in many expressions. (Some grammarians call these phrasal forms of the verb).

> The reporter did not make up the story.
> The editor woke up the reporter.
> The student refused to fill out the form.

Up and *out* aren't prepositions in those sentences. *Up the story, up the reporter* and *out the form* aren't prepositional phrases. Read the sentences again, and you'll see that *up* and *out* are closely tied to the verbs *make, woke* and *fill.* Remember that you do not put hyphens in these verb forms.

> *Not:* The student planned to set-up his exhibit the next morning.
> *But:* The student planned to set up his exhibit the next morning.

> *Not:* The factory will lay-off 20 workers.
> *But:* The factory will lay off 20 workers.

Hyphens, ages and dimensions. Ages and dimensions are hyphenated as adjectives in front of nouns. (Note: The AP uses numbers with ages.)

> The 10-year-old boy was accused of stealing.
> The 4-year-old company has never made a profit.
> A 7-foot-tall center is on the coach's wish list.
> The man survived a 300-foot fall into the East River.
> A 12-inch blanket of dust covered his desk.

Ages and dimensions are not hyphenated in these uses:

> The boy who was accused of stealing is 10 years old.
> The company, which is 4 years old, has never made a profit.
> The coach wishes he had a center who was 7 feet tall.
> The man fell 300 feet into the East River.
> His desk was covered by 12 inches of dust.

Ages and dimensions are hyphenated when used as nouns:

> The 14-year-old will be tried as an adult.
> The 76-year-old ran the fastest mile of the day.
> The law does not allow 14-year-olds to marry.
> The 7-footer did not have to jump to dunk the ball.

EXERCISE 35   NAME _____

Practice exercise. Answers in back of book.

Put hyphens and commas where they're needed and correct any misspellings. You may need to check the *AP Stylebook* and a dictionary.

1. The mismanaged bookstore allegedly had not paid federal taxes for the past five years.

2. The well dressed attorney walked quickly from the meeting and said he would never return.

3. Unruly fans angrily booed the referees and frequently threw cups of beer onto the basketball court.

4. Neither the workers nor the company is willing to discuss the yearlong strike.

5. A steady downpour drenched the bone dry city and tied up rush hour traffic.

6. Police said the hold up man ordered the bank guard to lay down his weapon.

7. The out of work man said he needed a part time job to buy Christmas presents.

8. His wife works full time at a motel that pays notoriously low wages.

9. The burly 310 pound lineman called the report a "set up job by good for nothing reporters."

10. The senator proposed a bill that would allow 18 year olds to drink beer.

11. The coroner said the three month old baby had a six inch slash across her back.

12. The Cincinnati based company paid 12 year old boys to sell the second rate candy door to door.

13. The gangsters planned to walk out of prison and head for their hide out.

14. The doctor apologized to the worried man and said there was a mix up in the records.

15. The doctor said the man's check up did not indicate that he was headed for a mental break down

    after all.

16. The overrated medic said the xrays were upside down when he very hurriedly glanced at them.

17. The doctor said he was completely embarrassed by the first mistake he had made in his long distin-

    guished career. "I've behaved like a silly incompetent intern," he said.

18. The patient who was much too angry to talk reached into the pocket of his blue double breasted suit

    and pulled out a business card.

19. He tried to steady his violently shaking hand before handing the brightly colored card to the doctor.

20. The card identified the patient as a personal injury attorney who specialized in medical malpractice.

EXERCISE 36   NAME _____

Put hyphens and commas where they're needed in the following sentences and correct the spelling. You will need to check the *AP Stylebook* as you do this exercise.

1. An out of state company plans to tear down the houses and build a shopping center.

2. The mall will have more brand name stores and will attract a wealthier clientele than other malls in the area according to a representative for the company.

3. Neither the owner of the property nor neighbors were willing to discuss the settlement.

4. The planning commission will hear objections to the mall at its meeting in January but will delay its final decision until after the elections in November.

5. A 6 foot tall driver may feel cramped in the company's new sports cars.

6. An appeals court overturned a 3 year old law that requires children to be 14 years old before they can work in fast food restaurants.

7. The bookstore admitted its prices were excessively high.

8. The tired sweaty athletes said they wanted to be alone.

9. Schools in small towns receive less state aid per student than their big city counterparts.

10. The breakin at the computer store in the newly remodeled student union surprised police.

11. The walkout ended when the company agreed to rehire the laid off workers.

12. The out of court settlement allowed offshore drilling to continue.

13. The Blasters outscored the Trojans in the season ending contest for both teams.

14. The children had first degree burns over most of their bodies.

15. State inspectors reminded the owner that flour should be stored in a cool dry place.

16. The big city lawyer meekly admitted he had been tricked by the small town prosecutor according to a front page story in *The Tribune*.

17. The tired soot covered firefighters fought bravely to breathe life back into the six month old.

18. They were obviously grateful when medics arrived to takeover the rescue effort.

19. The fire chief knew the firefighters would suffer a letdown when they heard that the baby was dead-on-arrival at Lakeview Hospital.

EXERCISE 37: A REVIEW   NAME _____

Correct any comma and style errors in these sentences. Make sure who, whom, that and which are used correctly.

1. The FBI arrested the Boise Idaho man on July 16 2001 on charges of raping three women in Helena Montana in April 1999 and killing a police officer in Vail Colorado on May 2 2000.

2. Police found several bags of pot in the trunk of his car and 3 marijuana plants growing in the window of his apartment.

3. Doris Wilson who covers telecommunications for the *Tribune* said she used the Internet to track down a copy of the bill and to get the reactions of several Senators and media experts.

4. "We had time to save only one of them" the doctor said "and I had to decide quickly."

5. The National Guard which has seen action in several flood zones in the past will help search for missing children in the Mojave Desert which is one of the driest places on earth.

6. Director Hector Silva's film "Slim Chances" made millions of dollars but his latest effort "Fingerprints of God" is a flop at the box office.

7. Since Republican Maria Sanchez was elected to the City Council last year she has won the support of both Republicans and Democrats.

8. Party regulars are trying to persuade her to run for mayor since she is the party's most popular candidate.

9. Howard Smith became president of Northern State University on December 10 1964 and resigned on January 3 1965 the shortest tenure of any NSU president.

10. Judge Susan Brown on Tuesday fined attorneys Jay Hoover and Dewey Rich $500 for arriving 15 minutes late to a hearing and told them that she would double the fine if they were late again.

11. Northern Cablevision's rates for 45 channel service will go up 20 percent on August 20 but rates for customers that receive the basic package will go down 5 percent.

12. NSU Vice President Kathleen Devine said that tuition for graduate classes will double next year and that undergraduate classes will cost 40 percent more.

13. Jane Summers who resigned last week as principal of Central High School has taken a job with Associated Education Inc. which designs software programs for schools.

14. The company which does not get the contract to build jets for Delta will go out of business.

15. Police suspect the men who robbed the First National Bank on July 10th were also responsible for bank robberies in Muncie Indiana and Celina Ohio in May.

16. Northern Cablevision which serves most of the dormitories on Northern's campus said Tuesday it will raise rates by 20 percent.

17. Western's Bulldogs lost to Eastern State in the consolation round of the NCAA playoffs 8-3.

18. In the first round of the NCAA playoffs the Northern State Blasters defeated the Southern State Trojans 65-14.

19. Although 10 students saw the crime none of them called police.

20. The registrar accidentally erased the computer records of students who registered early for classes.

21. "How many more must die by the hands of their spouses before the church gets involved" Jackson asked.

22. Nelson said he wondered how many people must die on the highways before the legislature will require prison sentences for all drunk driving convictions.

23. "How many of you have read my article titled "Journalism's Future"," the professor asked the class.

24. Because the police officers knew Ruby they allowed him to cross police lines.

25. The minister said he stole money from the church because he owed gamblers $10,000.

26. The senator asked the crowd to count the number of promises that his opponent had broken.

27. The mayor was 'drunk beyond belief' one eyewitness told police.

28. Florence Baker who told police she saw the murder testified that she could not identify the man who pulled the trigger.

EXERCISE 38: A REVIEW   NAME _____

Put hyphens and commas in the following sentences and make sure the subjects and verbs and the nouns and pronouns agree. Correct the lie-lay and who-whom problems and all style errors.

1. The newly elected mayor said there would be no letdown in his efforts to solve the city's woes.

2. A front page story in the student run newspaper reported that the university offered Bill Williams, the 65 year old coach of the NSU baseball team, a 10 year contract.

3. Because of a mixup in construction orders workers accidentally tore down the 104 year old gymnasium instead of a parking garage that the university abandoned five years ago.

4. Police said the hold up men tried to break out of the county jail by digging through its crumbling walls. The building is more than 200 years old.

5. Police said the suspects fled in a rusty pick-up truck but were later seen in a brand new sports car.

6. Although Jenkins applied for a part time job, the editor was so impressed with his performance on the newspaper's editing exam that she hired him full time.

7. Daniels Shoe Co. Tuesday announced that they will shutdown their Main Street store.

8. The little known actor stole the show with his incredibly realistic characterization of a writer who was a heavy user of heroin.

9. The attorney said the brothers should not be required to spend the rest of their life in prison.

10. The Academic Standards Committee, composed of both professors and students, told the coach they needed to talk to the player himself.

11. Ace Moldings Corp. will hire 100 new employees for their Amesville plant next month.

12. The library requires all students to show their identification card before they can borrow books.

13. The museum's policy of not exhibiting their best known paintings disappoints first time visitors.

14. The Indians will no longer play their home games in Municipal Stadium.

15. A group of angry students have demanded that the college change the way they hire professors.

16. Northern State University, along with 15 universities in five states, plan to appeal the decision.

17. The laid off workers said the company should offer them a job in another of its factories.

18. Either the company or the workers are not telling the truth.

19. He was fined ten dollars for throwing rocks at a dog that was laying in his flower bed.

20. Neither the attorneys nor the judge was expecting the jury to return so quickly.

21. Looking for new ways of making money, the Internet has become a tool for both savvy entrepreneurs and shabby con artists.

22. Many people buy three year memberships in health clubs and gyms but they stop going to them after a few months.

EXERCISE 39: A REVIEW   NAME _____

PART 1

Put hyphens and commas in the following sentences and make sure that the subjects and verbs and the nouns and pronouns agree. Correct any style errors. (Some sentences may already be correct.)

1. Twenty percent of the faculty have degrees from European universities.

2. Forty percent of the engineering students are women and most of them say they expect no discrimination when they begin their careers.

3. Although Garrity was a first year law student, she scored average marks on the exam.

4. Still exhausted from the campaign the newly elected president began to select his cabinet.

5. The county library system plans to relocate their branch in the Parkland Mall to the recently opened Mercury Plaza on Fifth Street.

6. After arguing heatedly over the budget for three hours, the City Council voted to end their meeting with a prayer for friendship and understanding.

7. Less than a year ago the mall lay in shambles with its windows boarded-up. However, today it's filled with brightly colored shops advertising brand name clothes at discount prices.

8. After pulling the 19 year old man from a recycling bin behind a restaurant on Main Street police charged him with armed robbery.

9. Organizers gave students attending the state band contest a certificate to take back to their schools.

10. One 12 year old was so excited when they called his name to receive a certificate that he ran onto the stage and tripped over a flower pot.

11. The majority of antiabortion protesters outside the Lakeside Women's Clinic that opened last week was peaceful. However, a small group of them were arrested for disobeying police orders to leave.

12. A 5 year old girl was in critical condition after she fell from a window in the 10 story building.

13. The Lewiston Indiana company has made chocolate covered cherries for 120 years.

14. He was born on Feb. 12, 1958 in Salem Oregon and began logging in 1976.

15. The campus chapter of the Society of Professional Journalists will sell AP Stylebooks to raise money to send their officers to the national SPJ convention next fall.

16. Neither the workers nor the company were interested in the president's proposal.

17. The workers and the company has agreed on arbitration.

18. The Republican Party expects 10,000 people to attend their convention in Branson Missouri Monday.

19. After being fined four times in five years Consolidated Chemical has promised to reduce the amount of pollution created by their paper mills.

20. Although the 82 year old had never been in trouble with the law before witnesses identified him as the holdup man who robbed three liquor stores last week.

21. Winners of the Super Bowl receive a ring and a large bonus.

PART 2

Make sure that lie, lay, who and whom are used properly in these sentences.

22. Whoever wins the election will need to deal with the economy.

23. Whoever the voters choose will need to deal with the economy.

24. The best students usually take jobs with whoever offers them the most money.

25. The professor was surprised at how few students knew who wrote "Moby-Dick."

26. By tradition, contest judges are not allowed to say who they voted for.

27. The detective said police had no idea who the killer was.

28. The body was found lieing in a pool of blood on busy 11th Street.

29. Police said she had laid there for at least 10 hours before anyone called 911.

30. The cat lay in the street as if it were daring motorists to hit it.

31. Under the company's new cleanliness policy, anything left laying on desktops will be destroyed.

32. The gunman ordered tellers to lay on the floor.

33. Police ordered the men to lay their guns down and to lie on the ground with their legs apart.

34. The food laid just out of the reach of the starving prisoners until they agreed to confess.

35. To stop trucks from entering the plant, union members threw themselves in front of the trucks' tires and lay there until police arrived.

CHAPTER 5

SYNTAX

SECTION 1: USING WORDS AND PHRASES CORRECTLY

English has a very rich vocabulary and provides us with the opportunity to choose just the right word to express our ideas. The downside is that so many of our words have such subtle nuances in meaning that copy editors often run into words and phrases that are used imprecisely. If these editors aren't sure about these words and phrases, they look them up. You should, too.

The first place to look is in the *Associated Press Stylebook*. If what you need isn't there, try *Webster's New World Dictionary*. It's the standard desk reference at most news organizations.

Use your dictionary for more than spelling. Dictionaries list synonyms and discuss idiomatic usage of many words. You may find a word that would better suit the story. Keep a thesaurus handy, too.

Become familiar with other guides such as *The Elements of Style* by Strunk and White or any of Theodore M. Bernstein's books including *The Careful Writer, Headlines and Deadlines* and *Watch Your Language*. You might prefer newer books such as *Working With Words* by Brian Brooks and James Pinson or *When Words Collide* by Lauren Kessler and Duncan McDonald. They provide a much more thorough discussion of grammar and word usage than you'll find in general editing texts.

A poorly placed modifier can make a sentence have two meanings:

Students who cheat frequently were expelled from school.

Does the sentence mean that the school frequently expelled students who were caught cheating? Or does it mean that students had to be caught cheating many times before they would be expelled?

Guard against non sequiturs, which are modifiers that don't seem related to the sentence:

Non sequitur: Born in Indiana, Jones became a skilled mountain climber.
Related: Born in Utah, Jones became a skilled mountain climber.
Related: Born in Indiana, Jones had played basketball all her life.

Non sequitur: An accomplished mathematician, Jones refused to eat Twinkies.
Correct: An accomplished mathematician, Jones taught statistics to the other reporters.
Or: A health enthusiast, Jones refused to eat Twinkies.

Reporters sometimes write non sequiturs because they are trying to pack too much information into a sentence.

Born in Montana, Jones has a wicked curve ball.

Being from Montana has little to do with pitching. The editor might see whether Jones' birthplace might fit better somewhere else in the story.

Parallelism requires that words connected by conjunctions such as *and* and *or* be in the same grammatical form. In the first example that follows, *reading novels* is a participle phrase and *Nintendo* is a noun. The sentence can be made parallel by using either two participle phrases or two nouns:

Not: Reading novels (*phrase*) and Nintendo (*noun*) kept the team busy on the long bus ride.
Two phrases: Reading novels and playing Nintendo kept the team busy on the long bus ride.
Or two nouns: Novels and Nintendo kept the team busy on the long bus ride.

Another example:

Not: The ordinance would allow police officers to ask people for their phone numbers (*noun*) and where they lived (*clause*).
Two nouns: The ordinance would allow police officers to ask them for their phone numbers and addresses.
Or two clauses (grammatically correct but wordy): The ordinance would allow police officers to ask them what their phone numbers were and where they lived.

EXERCISE 40   NAME _____

Practice exercise. Answers in back of book.

PART 1

Select the preferred wording. Check with the *AP Stylebook* first. If you can't find the answer there, try a good dictionary. The answers are in the back of the book.

1. He was (arrested for, charged with) shoplifting.
2. She was (sentenced to, sentenced with) 10 years in a federal (prison, jail).
3. He was (convicted of, convicted with) petty theft.
4. She (suffered, received) injuries to the head and arms.
5. The car (collided with, crashed into) a (cement, concrete) wall.
6. She is an (alumnus, alumna, alumni) of Northern State University.
7. (Since, Because) he had the day off, he decided to watch the Rose Bowl game.
8. (Since, Because) his parents earned $60,000 a year, he could not apply for the scholarship.
9. His decision will (affect, impact on) wheat prices.
10. The play (centered on, centered around) man's need to be loved.
11. The university's (fiscal, physical) year ends in June.
12. The police officer (persuaded, convinced) the distraught man to drop the rock.
13. A good sales agent can (persuade, convince) the customer to buy all the extras.
14. The coach (convinced, persuaded) the university that athletes need special housing.
15. For (awhile, a while), the school board wanted to prohibit teachers (to speak, from speaking) about controversial issues.
16. The prime minister said his country was a (backward, backwards) nation that needed American (aid, aide) to survive.
17. The mayor is better-prepared (than, then) she was before.
18. Work was (underway, under way) on the new building when workers discovered the grave.
19. Some reporters read stories back to sources to (insure, ensure) the stories are accurate.

PART 2

Correct errors in modifier placement, parallelism, style, spelling and word usage. Some sentences may be correct.

20. Parents with incomes of more than $40,000 and who own their own homes cannot receive tuition rebates.

21. All Jackson wanted out of life was to play in the NFL and a red Porsche sports car.

22. People who go on fad diets frequently suffer muscle loss.

23. Despite the number of complaints, the company only promised to recall 100 cars.

24. The coach promised the alumni association he'd fill the stadium and a conference championship.

25. After praying for peace, the pope visited the hospital and talked to many wounded soldiers.

26. Based in Texas, the company is the nation's largest producer of salsa.

27. A native of Arizona, the new school superintendent promised to insure that every high school student received extensive training in computer science.

EXERCISE 41   NAME _____

Select the preferred wording. Check with the *AP Stylebook* first. If you can't find the answer there, try a good dictionary. (Most newspapers use *Webster's New World*.)

1. The nation is heading (towards, toward) socialism, the candidate said.

2. The child (drowned, was drowned) in the family pool on July 4.

3. The workers (hanged, hung) the painting in the president's office.

4. A Longwood company markets (a unique, the most unique) line of chocolates.

5. (A mediator, An arbitrator) will try to settle the dispute by finding a compromise that both sides will

   (accept, except).

6. The City Council (approved, passed) an amendment to the city charter.

7. The disgruntled man plans to (emigrate, immigrate) from the United States.

8. In her speech, Provost Marcella Jones (implied, inferred) that the university would raise tuition.

9. The burglar (ransacked, ramsacked) the apartment and (rifled, riffled) through the family's files.

10. The flag in front of the police station was at (half-staff, half-mast) in honor of the fallen officers.

11. After hearing the warnings about raw oysters, many diners now (forego, forgo) them.

12. (Beside, Besides) Jane, Viceroy has a daughter from an earlier marriage.

13. The youth was (arrested for, charged with) (drunk, drunken) driving.

14. He (pled, pleaded) guilty (to, of, for) (wreckless, reckless) driving.

15. He sent the package (partial, parcel) post.

16. (Since, Because) weather conditions were (averse, adverse), NASA postponed the launch.

17. The doctor did not think the disease would (re-occur, reoccur, recur).

18. The new proposal was considerably different (than, from) the earlier one.

19. He worked for a tool-and-(dye, die) company.

20. The astronauts resorted to using (duck, duct) tape to fix their vehicle.

21. The (principal, principle) reason for the change was to allow more students to attend football games.

22. (Fewer than, Less than) 200 students will receive financial (aid, aide).

23. Students would have (fewer, less) problems if they talked with their (advisers, advisors).

24. The couple's monthly payments, including (principal, principle) and interest, were $400.

25. When police looked (further, farther) into Wilson's past, they discovered some troubling things.

26. After being charged with theft, Williamson (paid, posted) bail and was released from (jail, prison).

27. The (affect, effect) of raising tuition is likely to be that (less, fewer) students can attend.

28. The new editor decided to (affect, effect) many changes in the design of the paper.

29. The City Council (passed, approved, adopted) an ordinance requiring motorists to turn down their radios.

30. Although he was (reared, raised) in a (healthy, healthful) family, he showed (antisocial, anti-social) tendencies.

31. Jackie Henry, (who's, whose) first book was (titled, entitled) *Frocks*, will speak Tuesday.

32. The (capital, capitol) of Tennessee is Nashville. (It's, Its) in the middle of the state.

33. The candidates will debate taxes on (capital, capitol) gains during (there, their, it's, its) first debate.

34. (They're, There, Their) also going to discuss a federal sales tax.

35. (It's, Its) likely that most people will see (they're, there, their) taxes go up.

36. (Less than, Fewer than) 45 (pickets, picketers) opposed to (capital, capitol) punishment marched in front of the (Capital, Capitol) in Washington and shouted insults at tourists (who's whose) (buses, busses) paused in front of the building.

37. The firefighter (dived, dove) into the water and tried to rescue the child. Despite his efforts, the child (drowned, was drowned).

38. Three students were (already, all ready) on the bus when the trip was (canceled, cancelled).

39. The mayor and her (aid, aide) had been very (discrete, discreet) about their affair.

40. The mayor tried to (disassociate, dissociate) herself from the unpopular governor.

41. The injured man told police he was (all right, alright), but he was later found (lying, laying) in the street (unconscious, unconscience).

42. Police said the teens were driving (backward, backwards) down Main Street (toward, towards) Central High School when their car (collided with, crashed into) a stalled dump truck.

SECTION 2: DANGLING MODIFIERS

Don't leave participle phrases dangling. Often participle phrases serve as the modifiers. When they do, they must be adjacent to the words they modify. They cannot be left dangling at the beginning of the sentence, as in this:

Having lowered its prices, customers are waiting in line to shop at Sears.

The phrase *Having lowered its prices* describes Sears, not the customers who shop there. You can fix this in two ways. You can rewrite the sentences so that the phrase is closer to the noun it modifies:

Having lowered its prices, Sears now has customers waiting in line to shop there.

Or you can rewrite the sentence and turn the phrase into a clause:

After Sears lowered its prices, customers had to wait in line to shop there.

Here are some more dangling phrases:

Not: Having been convicted of child molestation, the judge ordered Blakeley to stay away from children.
But: Having been convicted of child molestation, Blakeley was ordered to stay away from children.
Or: Because Blakeley had been convicted of child molestation, the judge ordered him to stay away from children.

Not: After receiving his MBA from Harvard, many companies offered him high-paying jobs.
But: After receiving his MBA from Harvard, he was offered many high-paying jobs.
Or: After he received his MBA from Harvard, many companies offered him high-paying jobs.

Not: After mixing the batter until it is smooth, nuts and chocolate chips are added.
But: After mixing the batter until it is smooth, add nuts and chocolate chips. (The subject *you* is understood.)
Or: After the batter is mixed until it is smooth, nuts and chocolate chips are added.

EXERCISE 42   NAME _____

Practice exercise. Answers in back of book.

Revise any of the following sentences that have dangling modifiers. Make sure that the punctuation and hyphenation are correct.

1. Trying to keep pace with its rapid growth Northern State University announced plans on Tuesday for four new residence halls.

2. Having loved the book the movie was a major disappointment to fans of Clancy's novels.

3. After graduating from college a job was his next goal.

4. After slugging the police officer the woman escaped on a mountain bike.

5. Having been out of school for five years the attitudes of many of the students surprised her.

6. After lowering its admission standards more students were accepted by Buckley College this year.

7. Knowing the source of his problems he vowed never to drink again.

8. Having been identified by three witnesses police decided to charge Murphy with the crime.

9. Having agreed to testify against his friend charges against Wilson were dropped.

10. Blessed with warm sunny weather tourists flock to southern Spain.

11. Having two prior felony convictions Jefferson feared he would receive a life sentence.

12. Seeing the storm approaching referees ordered the players to leave the field.

13. Having arrived an hour late, the judge fined the attorney $100 for contempt of court.

14. After walking the first three batters the crowd cheered when Thompson finally threw a strike.

15. Having worked on the copy desk of my college newspaper copy editing appeals to me as a career.

16. Having a strong command of grammar copy editing is easy for Stewart.

17. After losing a costly suit to the worker's widow, more attention was focused on employee safety.

18. Hoping to increase attendance at home games, ticket prices were lowered.

EXERCISE 43   NAME _____

Correct errors in modifier placement, punctuation, parallelism, style, grammar, spelling and word usage. Some sentences may be correct. Add punctuation marks as needed.

1. Before getting their degrees schools should make sure students have basic computer skills.

2. Less than 100 students signed up this semester for Principals of Everyday Computing which is the easiest class in the Computer Science Department.

3. However other educators believe schools should beef-up their offerings in government.

4. The Center for American Studies contends that every student who graduates from high school should know the names of their Senators and what rights are included in the Bill of Rights.

5. Traveling at speeds up to 180 mph quaint villages flash by the windows of France's high speed trains.

6. Every nation seems to have their own customs and rules about train travel.

7. Before boarding trains in Italy tickets must be stamped by a machine on the station platforms.

8. Investors who read *Smart Money* unfailingly make more money than those who don't.

9. Born in Oklahoma Ziegler made his first million by the time he was 30.

10. A graduate of Oxford University Reynolds hoped the State Department would assign him to the American Embassy in London.

11. The retiring professor said he will fill his days with writing his autobiography and volunteer work with underprivileged children.

12. Buried under 5 feet of snow the airlines canceled all flights into the Denver airport.

13. The trustees decided not to grant pay raises which angered the faculty senate.

14. Party leaders hanged pictures of the dictator from every building.

15. After winning the lottery Janet Adams said she wanted a new Cadillac for herself and to set up a college fund for her children.

16. Although powered by a small diesel engine most drivers say the new Mercedes has enough acceleration to suit their needs.

17. Reporters are judged by their ability to write and whether they can find sources quickly.

18. Reporters who can write quickly get promoted.

19. The new editor plans a new design for the front page and to find ways to make the news more readable.

20. Before flooding the valley the graves of pioneers were moved to high ground.

21. The intern only interviewed one source for her story which angered her assignment editor.

22. Even the most superficial stories at least need two sources.

23. Born in rural Iowa Billingsly understood the plight of the family farmer.

24. Knowing her husband would be in prison for ten years Potter decided it was alright for her to use the internet to meet other men.

25. Knowing the source was lying the reporter decided not to write the story.

26. Flying into Portland the view of Mount Hood is breathtaking.

27. After being knocked unconscious for the eighth time the doctor told Kolowski he could never box again.

EXERCISE 44   NAME _____

Revise any sentences that have dangling modifiers.

1. After watching the Blasters lose their opener, some alumni demanded the firing of Coach Maurice Collins.

2. Having made two serious errors in his first story, editors were reluctant to assign stories to the intern.

3. Knowing the author did not grant interviews, the reporter decided to pose as a graduate student.

4. After reading the newspaper story, the mayor decided to call the editor.

5. After being named coach of the year by *Basketball Weekly*, the university gave Mo Collins a raise.

6. Having died in the line of duty, police throughout the state wore black armbands in remembrance of the officer.

7. Concluding that the evidence was collected illegally, the judge told prosecutors they could not use it.

8. Having suffered a severe stroke, doctors said it could be weeks before Mansfield could testify.

9. Responding to a poll by the campus newspaper, most students said they believe the university should make computers readily available to them 24 hours a day.

10. Before eating dinner, prayers were said by the students.

11. Not expecting a quiz over the reading assignment, Quincy did not do well.

12. Recognizing that the war was lost, black flags were flown over the castle.

13. The agency hoped the ad campaign would persuade male dieters to buy low-calorie dinners instead of just women.

14. Having a fully equipped kitchen on the plane, the family style meals were quickly devoured by the passengers.

15. Having finished his last meal, prison authorities led Smidley to the execution chamber.

16. Powered by a much larger engine, Petty's car had an unfair advantage.

SECTION 3: PUNCTUATION AND QUOTATION MARKS

Quotations can be presented in three ways.

Paraphrase or indirect quote: Jackson said he would use all his wealth to defeat the measure.
Partial quote: Jackson said he would use "every last penny I've got" to defeat the measure.
Direct quote: Jackson said, "I'll use every last penny I've got to keep this thing from ever becoming law."

If the quote is wordy or lame, copy editors may find it necessary to turn direct quotes into paraphrases.

Lame: Jackson said, "I suspect, well, I guess that the SEC will take or listen to, anyway, the advice of the IRS on this one."
Paraphrase: Jackson said he guessed the SEC would listen to the IRS's recommendations.

However, copy editors cannot create quotes, and they surely can't "improve" quotes by making them more sensational. They were not there and they don't know what was said.

Original: Jackson said the United States should give help to people in the plague area.
Bad editing: Jackson said, "The United States should give help to people in the plague area."
Worse editing: Jackson said, "We should take our blinders off and go help those people suffering from the plague."

The only time copy editors can add quotation marks is when the reporter clearly forgot one. In the following quotation, it is clear the second sentence is also a direct quote.

Original: "I know we can do well," the coach said. We have the best players and the best fans."
Edited: "I know we can do well," the coach said. "We have the best players and the best fans."

Commas and periods always go inside quotation marks. The rule applies with full quotes, partial quotes, titles, and so on.

Not: He called the verdict "pure, unadulterated hogwash".
But: He called the verdict "pure, unadulterated hogwash."

Not: Shirley Jackson wrote the short story "The Lottery".
But: Shirley Jackson wrote the short story "The Lottery."

Use commas with attribution when you have direct quotations:

O'Hara told his fans, "I like being here."
"I like being here," O'Hara told his fans.

But don't get carried away and use quotation marks and punctuation with indirect quotations (also called paraphrases). Indirect quotations look like this:

O'Hara told his fans he liked being here.
He liked being here, O'Hara told his fans.

Correcting grammar in quotes is controversial. Some journalists believe that quotes should never be modified. Others believe that it is common courtesy to recognize that spoken English is rarely as exact as written language. A compromise at many papers is this: If the grammar error is appropriate or sounds more like normal conversation, it is not corrected. If the grammar error is not typical of the speaker, it is corrected:

Unlikely to be corrected: When asked who was hiding in the truck, the witness said, "It was me." (Not the grammatically correct: "It was I.")
Probably not corrected: "They told me to lay down and close my eyes," the clerk said. "There's three guys with guns, so that's what I did."
More likely to be corrected: The dean of the law school said, "Local customs in India and, as it has been explained to me, Indian law is clear about this."

Use commas with attributions such as "according to." The following sentences are correct:

Four passengers on the bus were injured, according to police.
According to school officials, the teacher will be fired.

Commas aren't used with "according to" on those rare occasions when the phrase is essential to understanding the meaning of the sentence.

The coach said the game was not played according to the rules.

Use commas when attributions come after, but not before, a paraphrase:

Jackson said the Badgers look strong.
The Badgers look strong, Jackson said.

With multiple-sentence quotations, usually the attribution is part of the first sentence.

Not: "I like our chances. I think our line is as strong as theirs. I know our running backs are better," Jones said.
But: "I like our chances," Jones said. "I think our line is as strong as theirs. I know our running backs are better."
Or: Jones said: "I like our chances. I think our line is as strong as theirs. I know our running backs are better."

Use single quotation marks inside double quotation mark.

A witness said, "The teller ran out of the bank and yelled, 'We've been robbed. God help us, we've been robbed.'"
"When I pulled open the car door," the fireman said, "I heard a faint voice crying, 'Mommy.'"
"No eighth-grader should be required to read Shirley Jackson's short story 'The Lottery,'" the principal said.

Don't use single quotation marks for emphasis or to show ironic meanings.

Not: Lincoln dedicated his life to 'truth and justice for all.'
But: Lincoln dedicated his life to truth and justice for all.
Or, if it's a partial quote: Lincoln dedicated his life to "truth and justice for all."

Not: The Central High Bearcats 'clawed' their way into the finals.

But: The Central High Bearcats clawed their way into the finals.

Question marks go inside quotation marks when you are quoting the entire question.

"Can we apply for a loan?" the mayor asked.
The student asked, "Did I really flunk the final?"

However, question marks go after the quotation marks when only the final words of a sentence are being quoted:

Have you read "The Lottery"?

Fortunately, you won't see this one very often:

The professor asked, "Have you finished reading 'The Lottery'?"

EXERCISE 45   NAME _____

Practice exercise. Answers in back of book.

Correct the errors in handling quotations in these sentences. Also fix any errors in word usage, grammar, AP style and so on. Not all sentences have mistakes.

1. The coach said he will not start Williamson in the home opener.

2. Williamson said "my arm feels great. I'm ready to go."

3. The trainer, however, said, "I don't think he's ready." "We don't want to lose him for the season."

4. According to university records O'Hara never attended the school.

5. "Why did you lie about where you went to college" the prosecutor asked O'Hara.

6. "You had to have a degree to get a job with Consolidated Airlines. I knew I could fly the planes. So I just told them I had a degree. I didn't think it would matter in the long run," O'Hara answered.

7. The prime minister said the agreement could lead to 'peace in our time'.

8. The mayor said she decided to run again "after months of soul-searching and talks with my family."

9. "Why would anyone want to ride a bike without a helmet. We have people in the emergency room every week with severe head injuries that could have been prevented" the doctor said.

10. "Either the legislature gives us more money or we cut programs," NSU Pres. Richard Aster responded. "We can not continue as we are. We have raised student fees as high as the law allows and we've slashed the budget every way imaginable. I can't tell you all the ways that those cuts have effected the quality of our programs."

11. "The legislators must find more money for higher education, especially for NSU. If they don't we'll begin dropping whole areas of study."

EXERCISE 46   NAME _____

Correct the mistakes in use of quotation marks, word usage, modifier placement, punctuation and parallelism in these sentences.

1. Quarterback Trace Cox said he considered Buckley 'the meanest football team we'll play'.

2. "Those guys will talk trash all day long. They'll give you that extra push and they'll knee you whenever they can. Their pros at what I call "the stealth foul", the kind the refs never see," he said.

3. Having received less than 10,000 votes in the last election, party officials discretely told Johnson he would not be their nominee this year.

4. Jenkins told Stengle his arm was alright. "Let me face one more batter".

5. The mayor suggested banning trucks from First Street and the elimination of all traffic on Main Street on weekdays. She said the changes would not go into affect until summer.

6. Trying to reduce overcrowding, some journalism classes will be offered on Saturdays.

7. The abortion case was "the toughest, most draining trial of my life." "Everyday there were new challenges that tested everyone of the principals I live by", the attorney said.

8. "Men may mean one thing when they say the word "love", but to women the word has a much different meaning" the author of the popular self-help book said.

9. "Yuck" said the little girl after eating a chocolate covered ant at the county fair.

10. Girls' reactions to new foods are often different than boys, according psychologist Al Brown.

11. "No doubt about it" he stated. Its the worse day of my life."

12. Before setting bail, the judge wanted to know the man's criminal record and where he worked.

13. The police officer testified, "He whispered in my ear "Suzie shot me" and then he died."

14. Who wrote the short story "The Bear?"

15. William Faulkner wrote "The Bear", which Hollywood turned into a lousy movie.

EXERCISE 47: REVIEW EXERCISE   NAME _____

Don't rewrite these stories. Correct any grammar, spelling, punctuation and AP style errors. Don't revise any sentences to circumvent grammar and style questions. Abide by the custom of cleaning up grammar in quotes. Assume that the stories are the paper in Northern City, the home of NSU.

STORY 1

Northern State University's administration Tuesday completed their plans to buy the facilities of Associated Testing Labs Inc. despite the wide-spread fears that the buildings are unsafe.

Officials say the $13,500,000 purchase will allow the university to add laboratories for science and engineering classes. The facility which includes ten laboratories, twenty offices and four large meeting rooms is about one-half mile North of the university on McKinley Blvd.

NSU along with Wilson Community College and Turner Community College began to grow rapidly in the 90s. Officials at the three schools plan to share the laboratories.

The building became available 2 years ago when Associated Testing was forced to shutdown after losing their license to preform medical radiation tests. The EPA discovered several violations of their rules, including polluting ground water and failure to maintain adequate safety procedures.

The accusations of pollution and contamination has caused many students and faculty to question the safety of the facility. Last week The Northern State Blaster, the campus newspaper reported that they had evidence that toxic-wastes had been dumped on the site.

University officials dismissed the Blaster story.

"The hazard has been greatly exaggerated, NSU spokesman Paul Burgess said "we have a report from the state environmental agency labeling the site "open to continued development and utilization".

Burgess said NSU plans to clean-up any problems with contamination.

"We've been assured by our engineers that the area is safe. The building will provide a first rate facility for our students at a much lower cost then building a new science hall."

STORY 2

The man Blick Hall is named after was arrested Tuesday for shop-lifting a jacket from the Northern State University campus bookstore.

NSU police took Howard Blick, 32, to the Spring County jail where they booked him on felony theft charges. The crime is classified as a felony since the jacket is valued at more-than $100. He posted $500 bond and was released.

Police said 4 clerks told them they saw Blick put on a NSU jacket and leave without paying.

One clerk George Bledsoe said he recognized the man who stole the jacket.

"He spoke to my business law class just this morning" Bledsoe said. "My Professor called him a distinguished alumni and a top notch small business man."

Blick denied stealing anything. When police asked him about the jacket he told them that it had been given to him by Cynthia Rhodes who is chairman of the Sociology Department. He called the clerks "stupid jerks. They obviously mistook me for another shopper who looked like me."

The police officer who arrested Blick said he had no idea who he was arresting.

"He kept telling me he was a big time supporter of the university and that he knew President Aster. He said I would be sorry if I lay a hand on him" Sergeant Bruce Matterson said. I just told him to shut-up and come with me"

Blick, a Louisville, Kentucky native was recently described by Fortune magazine as a real life Horatio Alger. While a stdent at NSU he worked parttime for a Longwood realtor. After graduating in May, 1988, he began to invest in real estate in Spring county, and made a fortune.

The Fine Arts Building was renamed Howard Blick Hall on June 12 1994 after Blick.

CHAPTER **6**

EDITING THE HARD-NEWS STORY

SECTION 1: RIDDING COPY OF WORDINESS AND REPETITION

Wordiness and needless repetition waste space that could be used for more facts or stories.

If you have trouble spotting wordiness, try this: Go through the story with the sole purpose of trying to cut 20 or 30 words from it. Often when you concentrate just on wordiness, you'll find lots of examples that you otherwise would have missed.

Don't automatically cut the color. Even when you have to trim a story for space, don't cut all the details and lively writing that make it readable. If the content editor and the reporter have agreed that interesting anecdotes, effective transitions and descriptive passages help the story, the copy editor shouldn't slash them. Similarly, if the content editor and the reporter have agreed to use a clever lead, the copy editor shouldn't change it into a traditional summary lead.

Do as little harm to the story as possible. Nothing irritates a reporter—or a copy desk chief—more than a copy editor who places mistakes in a story or makes the writing choppy or disorganized. Reread every passage you change. You may find you have juxtaposed information in a way that is misleading or eliminated information necessary to give context to the story. You may have created "headless snakes" by eliminating the first reference to people who reappear later in the story and are called only by their last names. Or you may be guilty of "dumb mistakes" such as leaving words out or making grammatical errors.

Eliminating wordiness is different from trimming a story to fit a specific space. When you eliminate wordiness, you don't remove facts and information, just verbiage. Occasionally, you'll have to trim a locally written story for space, and you may have to cut information. Even then, you still try not to harm the story. Good editing means maintaining the reporter's voice and writing style.

EXERCISE 48   NAME _____

Practice exercise. Answers in back of book.

Edit the following briefs, paying particular attention to wordiness. You do not want to delete any information. You'll also find errors in grammar and AP style. Assume that the briefs are for an NSU campus newspaper. An edited version is in the back of your book. Remember that cutting stories requires some subjective decisions. You may find that we caught some things you missed. You may also decide that some of your changes are better than ours.

STORY 1

Journalism students at Northern State University won't be using new computers as soon as they had hoped. The journalism department on Monday rejected the only bid it received for the new equipment.

Professor Susan Pritchard said the department had hoped to replace the twenty aging computers in its graphics labs with state of the art equipment but had received only one bid from computer suppliers.

She said the department was forced to reject the sole bid because it was too high. She said they will readvertise for bids and that will delay the purchase of computers for several months.

STORY 2

Rodney Darwin, president of Citizens Bank, will be the speaker Saturday at the Tenth Annual Awards banquet for the Northern State University Economics Club.

Darwin will be the substitute speaker in place of Congressman William E. Greshaw. Mr. Greshaw will be unable to speak at the banquet because he will be in Washington attending the special session of congress.

EXERCISE 49   NAME _____

Edit the following briefs, paying particular attention to wordiness. You do not want to delete any information. You'll also find errors in grammar and AP style. Assume that the stories are for an NSU campus newspaper.

STORY 1

The editor of The Blaster, the Northern State student newspaper, said the paper is facing a critical shortage of cash which the paper must resolve by the end of the month if they are to have enough money to pay their printing costs.

Joyce Pulliam, whose in her second year as editor of the paper, said the paper will not issue checks to the employees who work for it and will ask Custom Printing, who prints the Blaster, to give them an extension so they can pay their printing bill late.

Pulliam said in two months it will receive a large payment from the sales agency that represents it in dealings with national advertisers. They pay the paper once a year for advertisements that have appeared in it.

"We'll be fine for the physical year as a whole, she said. But until that check comes in we're hurting."

STORY 2

Baseball is not the only Northern State University sport that has seen student support for their team fade in recent years, according to assistant athletic director Gretchen Kemp.

Men's basketball and both women's basketball and volleyball have fallen victim to the lack of student support. Kemp said that in the past these sports have made enough money to pay their own way. But this year the gate receipts will not cover their expenses because less students bought tickets.

She said declines in attendance were not uncommon on the nation's college campuses. "Many schools are in the same boat we're in," she said.

She said football was the only sport that had experienced gains in attendance from previous years.

STORY 3

The Northern State library has been told to look into ways to cutdown on the number of books that are stolen from the library.

NSU President Richard Aster asked Glen Hudson, chief librarian, to prepare a report for him by the end of next week with information about all books that have been stolen from the university's main library and the branch libraries, including their titles and subject matter.

Aster said he believed that students in certain majors were more likely to steal books from the library than were students in other majors and he wanted to find out why. He said he had been told that books about computers and books with copies of famous artworks were more likely to be stolen from the library than other books.

EXERCISE 50   NAME _____

Edit this story, paying particular attention to wordiness. In the margins, explain why you made the cuts. Don't forget to correct grammar, punctuation, spelling and style errors. Assume that the story is written for a paper in the city where NSU is.

If Marcella Jones was a student in American History II at Northern State University, she'd be flunking the course.

Fortunately for her, she's the teacher.

Jones is one of about a half-dozen or so administrators, who regularly teach classes. She teaches American History II at 7:30 a.m. on Monday, Wednesdays and Fridays.

So far she has missed more than 30 per cent of the classes this semester, said Amy Lerman, a graduate assistant who assists Jones with the class.

"One week she was gone for two days and came in a half an hour late on the third," said Stacey Schmitz, a junior History major. "There's a note on the door that day telling us to wait for her."

Jones said she only missed class on those days when her duties as provost required her to be out-of-town.

"I told the students up front that there would be times that I couldn't be there," she said. "In almost every instance, I was out of the state on university business and could not attend."

A provost is in charge of the academic aspects of the university and answers directly to the president.

Most students aren't bothered by Jone's absences.

"I haven't heard anyone grumbling," said Heather Kirkman, a senior majoring in journalism. "We understand that she has other things on her plate. I would have thought she would miss more."

Schmitz said that students understood that Jones had important things to do and didn't mind when she missed, mostly because they liked Jones.

However, students who miss Jone's class, didn't get by so easy. They are penalized because quizzes are given each class period over the reading material. Jones allows only two absences without a note from a doctor.

David Stern, a engineering major, said he liked the idea that the Provost was teaching a class, even if she missed often.

"I think it's good for a Provost to have hands on experience with NSU students. Some administrators have forgotten what student life is like."

Sally Anne Morris, History Department chairman, said she had heard nothing but good comments about Jones class. "She was a fine teacher before she became an administrator," Morris said. "Why shouldn't she be a good teacher now"?

Morris admitted that if a regular faculty member missed nearly a third of their classes, she would not be happy. "But we all know the demands placed on the provost."

Few NSU administrators teach classes, according to a check by a reporter last week. None of the university's seven deans were teaching this semester. According to university rules, each of them are required to teach one course every 2 years. President Astro has taught one class in his seven years at the helm of the university, and that was a three week seminar for school superintendents.

Department chairmen are asked to teach one class a year although many do not. Carl Young, chair of the English department admits he has'nt taught a class in four years. "This job has lots of responsibilities that place demands on my time," Dr. Young said. "I'd love to get back in the classroom more often. But, gosh, there's just no time."

SECTION 2: CONTENT EDITING

Leads must be supported by the story. Each idea raised in the lead normally is explained in greater detail in the story. If the lead raises questions that the story doesn't answer, the lead may need to be rewritten. Similarly, if much of the material in the story is not related to the lead, the editor should question whether the lead belongs in the story.

Leads must get readers into a story. Reporters and editors know that today's readers are very selective. Few of them will read a story if its lead does not catch their attention. Although reworking leads is best done by the reporter and the assignment editor, all editors should be on the lookout for dullness.

Editors must also guard against "hyped" leads. In their search for attention-grabbing leads, sometimes reporters go too far. Few papers want to trick people into reading their stories. Overstated leads are perhaps even worse than dull leads because they can mislead and misinform readers.

Anticipate readers' questions and make sure they're answered. Editors are often in better positions to spot holes in stories than reporters are. That's because reporters may know the information so well that they cannot see that their stories are missing details or background. But editors may not be as familiar with the facts. The questions they have about the story are likely to be the ones that readers would ask. Good editors make sure that those questions are answered. Sometimes that means asking the reporter to do some more checking.

Transitions are writing devices that shift the reader's attention from one aspect of the story to another. In journalistic writing, transitions can be individual words such as also, another and however or phrases and sentences such as "Many students, however, disagree with the president's decision." When the story is organized in blocks, transitions play an even more important role in making stories easy to read.

Trim surgically. Copy editors do not automatically cut off the bottom of a story if it is too long. Instead, they remove wordiness and repetition. They avoid mindlessly cutting all the color from the story because they know readers are unlikely to stay with a story that is boring. And they preserve the transitions that keep the story from seeming disjointed, choppy or even unintelligible.

Assignment editors coach reporters. They give help and guidance while the reporters are gathering information and writing their stories. After the reporter has finished a draft of the story, the assignment editor and reporter discuss it.

EXERCISE 51   NAME _____

Practice exercise. Answers in back of book.

Assignment 1. Assume that you're a content editor of the daily paper in the small city where Northern State University is. Your reporters turned these stories in two hours before deadline. What information would you want them to add to these stories? Remember that each reporter has only 90 minutes or so to gather the information you request.

Assignment 2. Correct all the style, grammar, spelling and other errors in the stories.

STORY 1

Four people were taken into custody Tuesday evening when police raided the Gamma Delta Iota   1.

fraternity house.   2.

Arrested were James McAfee, 19, William Ramsey, 20, Clinton DeFord, 18, all residents of the   3.

fraternity house, and Sally Anne Jennings, 45, 211 S. Jefferson St.   4.

Northern City Police Capt. Janet Long said neighbors of the fraternity house called police com-   5.

plaining about a party in the back yard of the fraternity house at 324 University Blvd.   6.

STORY 2

Northern State university President Richard Aster apologized Tuesday for the university's han-   7.

dling of an NSU student who wrote a letter critical of the university to the *Springdale Chronicle*.   8.

Aster told a standing room only crowd at a NSU student senate meeting that he did not intend to   9.

intimidate the student.   10.

"A president throwing his weight around is the kind of thing that can chill discussion on a uni-   11.

versity campus," Aster said, "I never want to be looked upon as a president who limited freedom of   12.

expression on campus."   13.

Aster had planned to discuss several bills pertaining to higher education currently being debated   14.

by the legislature.   15.

Instead, he responded to a resolution that the student senate past last week demanding he apolo-   16.

gize to the student. The student was questioned by high ranking university officials after the letter   17.

appeared in the *Chronicle*. According to the senate's resolution, university police checked his   18.

criminal record and credit history.   19.

Aster said he had written a letter to Claude Raines, a junior majoring in engineering, and apolo-   20.

gized. He assured Raines the incident would not be part of his school record.   21.

STORY 3

A four-poster bed valued at more than $250,000 was stolen Tuesday night from Ye Old Town   22.

Antiques Shoppe at Main and Jackson Streets.   23.

Police said that burglars cut their way through a metal door in the alley behind the store and car-   24.

ried out the bed. Molly Ervin, owner of the shoppe, said no other items appeared to have been stolen   25.

and the thieves took no money from the shop's safe.   26.

"This has all the markings of a professional job," Detective Dan Young said. "They used a   27.

sophisticated way of getting through that rear door. They knew the item they wanted. They got in   28.

smoothly, got the item they were looking for and then got out. I bet the whole job took them less   29.

than 5 minutes."   30.

The bed was to be a featured item at an auction at the shoppe this Saturday.   31.

EXERCISE 52   NAME _____

Assignment 1. You may find that important information has been omitted from these stories, the facts are inconsistent or the leads are not supported. If you were the assignment editor and 90 minutes remained before the deadline, what would you tell the reporters they need to do to improve these stories? Remember that you'll lose the respect of your reporters if your questions lack focus or demand extensive reporting without concern for deadlines. Assume that the stories are for a Northern City daily.

Assignment 2. Edit the stories for style, grammar, word usage and punctuation errors and eliminate any wordiness.

STORY 1

A former president of Northern State University was charged with drunken driving, assault on a police officer, and reckless driving Tuesday night in downtown Northern City.

Officer Kurt Williams said he saw Dobson Jennings, 45, 21 Kings Way, drive erratically from the parking lot of the Hitching Post Tavern and pulled him over.

Williams said Jennings became belligerent. When Williams asked him to take a sobriety test, Jennings punched Williams in the face, knocking the officer to the ground.

Jennings then got back in his car, put it in gear and rammed Williams patrol car, according to Officer Janet Voss, who arrived at the scene to back-up Williams. Voss took Jennings to the county jail, where he refused to take a breath-alcohol test.

Officer Williams received a broken nose and a deep cut over his eye. He was treated at University Hospital.

STORY 2

A chain-reaction accident near the Northern City Mall shut down traffic on busy Washington Boulevard and knocked power out for more than 1,000 homes late Monday night.

At least 10 cars were damaged in the accident, but no one was seriously injured.

Police said a car driving by Marty Potter, 61, 275 N. 9th St., stopped at a red light at Washington and 25th Street, touching off the pile-up.

Four cars were considered total losses and five others had to be towed from the scene.

Police said the accident was weather-related.

STORY 3

Much to the disappointment of Southside High basketball coach Sam Lewis, his Raiders did not crack the state's Top Ten list this week. The Raiders were one of five teams given honorable mention.

The Raiders, 10–2 for the season and 4–1 in conference play, put on two impressive showings last week. They upset third-ranked Spring Central, 70–69, in overtime and defeated 10th-ranked Lewiston, 65–62. Spring Central fell to number 9 this week. Lewiston was replaced by Ashbourne in the 10th spot.

The undefeated Tipton Blue Devils remained the top-rated team in the state, with Halstead second. The rest of the top ten were 3. Brookline, 4. Jackson, 6. Overton, 7. Washington Central and 8. Hobbs Valley.

STORY 4

A 79-year-old woman on Monday filed a $1 million suit against the Northern City Steak and Ribs Place restaurant.

Her attorney, Dorothy Wilson, said the suit is the first under the state's new civil liability statutes, which went into effect last month.

"The reformed laws shifts the burden of proof to make these kinds of suits more equitable," Wilson said. "In the past we would have had to prove that the business was totally to blame before our client could get any retribution. Now the law allows "shared responsibility" which means that we can collect those portions of the damages that resulted from the restaurant's negligence."

Bob Mooreland, the restaurant's attorney, said he had not seen the suit but said he was familiar with the case. "I think it's best if I wait to comment until we see how this thing develops," Mooreland said. "Believe me, the Nussbaum family, who owns the restaurant, want a fair settlement here. There's no bad guys here."

No court date has been set.

EXERCISE 53   NAME _____

A content editor would want some additional information added to this story. Identify what questions the reporter needs to answer. Also, edit the story for grammar, style, punctuation and so on.

The former director of Northern State University's educational support department stole cash and took home thousands of dollars worth of electronic equipment, according to accusations in a university investigation report.

Belinda Marger, 49, resigned in April after Provost Marcella Jones recommended to the Regents she be fired after working 22 years for the university.

Details of the investigation was released Tuesday after a public records request by The Blaster, the NSU student newspaper.

The investigation into Marger's conduct was sparked by complaints from a employee in the department that he suspected illegal activities.

Marger could not be reached for comment Tuesday.

According to the university report, the unnamed employee told a university official that Marger went with him to Home Depot in July of last year and purchased about $1,000 worth of supplies, most of which was taken to Marger's home. Among those items taken to her home, he said, was three ceiling fans. He said he hung one in her kitchen and two on an outside patio.

"She told me, Don't you say anything to anyone, because if you do, I'm through with you," the employee is quoted as telling officials.

When confronted by university officials, the accusations were denied. Marger said the employee was lying in an attempt to get back at her for telling him he needed to work harder, the report said.

"He wasn't a happy camper about that," she said in the report.

On another occasion the employee said an overhead TV projection system had been sent to a local shop for repairs. When the repairs completed, Marger told him to pick up the system and take it to her son-in-laws house. He said the device was listed on university records for months as being in the shop. "I know because we were getting lots of calls from pushy professors wanting to know when that thing would be back in the lecture hall," the employee was quoted as saying. It was not returned until the start of classes in the fall, he said.

Once investigators began questioning Marger about such practices, she returned a 27-inch TV and a number of other school items, including a lap-top computer, a digital camera, a scanner, a pager, a cell-phone, two Palm Pilots and a calculator, the report said.

Marger produced documents showing that she had signed out some of the items for temporary use. On the receipts were the initials of her secretary Mayra Hernandez. Hernandez later told university officials that Marger had her sign the receipts after the district started looking into Marger's activities, not before. Hernandez told her that she was 'trying out the equipment at home to make sure it worked OK'.

EXERCISE 54   NAME _____

A content editor would want some additional information added to this story. Identify the questions that the reporter needs to answer. Then edit the story for grammar, style, punctuation and so on.

Every student's dreams may have come true at Lincoln High School—for a short time any way.

School officials acknowledged Tuesday that two students had hacked their way into the school's computer and were changing classmate's grades for five dollars.

Now diplomas and college entrance paperwork is being delayed while teachers reexamine all the grades of the 2,500 students at the school.

Two students, described as "computer whizzes," have been accused of violating the student code of conduct regulating technology that forbids "vandalizing data [and] infiltrating systems," officials said.

School officials said grade transcripts will not include grades from this year until all grades have been checked by teachers. This may be a hard ship for college bound seniors. They must provide up to date transcripts to universities they would like to attend.

Graduation may be delayed if the grade checks are not completed in time according to school officials.

"This is a serious matter, and it must be dealt with seriously," a school district spokesman said.

One suspect's parents said their son was being accused of 'completely-bogus' charges. Parents of the other boy said there son only provided computer help to friends, and but did not change grades himself.

School officials would not release the boys names because they are 14 years old. This papers policy is to not name minors accused of serious crimes unless they are tried in adult court rather than in the juvenile justice system.

District investigators are trying to determine whether other students were involved, said Joe Melita, executive director of the district's investigative unit.

No one knows how many records were changed, but at least twenty student have admitted to paying $5 to have grades changed, Assistant Principal Patricia Browne said.

But all teachers were asked in a memo Tuesday to 'review your grades in previously saved documents'.

Two years ago, Lincoln High became a test facility for a centralized computer system called the e-gradebook. Every grade, including test and quiz scores, are entered into the system by teachers. The system is designed to provide guidance councilors and other school administrators will up to date information on students progress.

When the system was installed, representatives of Jude's Software boosted that the system was a "the most secure system outside of the Pentagon." They said a combination of firewalls and passwords made it all but impossible to hack.

One student who asked to remain anonymous said that many students considered the statement a challenge. "Guys at the Computer Club said they could get in," he said. "They said it would take a couple of months maybe." The student said he did not know if any students were successful.

Clarence Kohbe, who teaches computer classes at the school, said he had heard student joke about breaking the system. "I took it to be a big joke," he said. "Some of the kids like to steal each others passwords and things like that, but I never thought they would try something like this."

Jose Jude, president of the software company, said he doubted anyone really hacked into the system. "More than likely," he said, "they found a list of teachers passwords or something like that. The system is too sophisticated for a 14 year old to break." The company plans to send one of their experts to Lincoln High to help school officials deal with the problem.

Kohbe said he suspected that the students may have found a way to hack into the school's computers and to get teacher's passwords.

They likely changed other students' grades, not their own, because they are "very, very smart kid," Brown said. "These are not your average students. "They've been around computers for a long time, have computers at home, and go to hacker [Web] sites to learn how to do this."

School officials received an anonymous tip from a student about grade changing some months ago.

"Some of our teachers said they had also heard talk," Browne said. "So we took the tip seriously. We questioned the boy accused by the anonymous tip and checked his grades. We couldn't find anything, and his grades were alright."

The investigation was re-opened last week when a teacher noticed that a zero she had given a student had been changed to a 100. When that student was questioned, he broke down and cried. He admitted he had paid a student $5 to change the grade. The student said he had heard about the grade change racket several weeks before.

CHAPTER **7**

OTHER WAYS TO TELL THE NEWS

The line between news stories and features has become blurred as newspapers hustle to find engaging ways of telling the news. Although traditional news stories with summary leads and the information arranged in order of importance are the mainstays of American journalism, many newspapers want reporters to produce writing that is more conversational and accessible. Often the result is that the stories emphasize the human element in the news.

These stories often have delayed leads. *Anecdotal leads* are one kind. They tell little stories that are funny, poignant or serious. They illustrate the story in human terms. Editors must make sure that anecdotal leads give an accurate impression of what the story is about. These leads may be written more like scenes from short stories and novels than traditional newspaper writing. Unlike summary leads, delayed leads are often three or four paragraphs long, and occasionally you'll encounter some that are even longer.

Nut grafs usually follow delayed leads. Nut grafs explain the point of the story and give it a focus. Nearly all stories benefit from a clear statement of what the story is about, but new approaches to news writing have made nut grafs even more important.

Overwriting and description that is not relevant to the point of the story are flaws frequently found in stories. Editors occasionally must remind writers that the aim is not to show off their observational powers but to give readers a more vivid understanding of events and the people involved in them. One test: Does the description help explain the point of the story, as presented in its nut graf?

Writers are often allowed to write with voice. Most traditional journalistic writing lacked individuality. Reporters shied away from descriptive phrases and from colorful writing for fear of introducing opinion. Today many newspapers want their reporters and feature writers to write with *voice*, to use slang and word plays just as they might in normal conversation.

These kinds of writing styles have placed greater responsibility on assignment editors and copy editors to make sure that the voice the reporter has used is appropriate. Editors must also be on guard for biases, which can slip into these stories.

EXERCISE 55   NAME _____

Practice exercise. Answers in back of book.

Assignment 1. If you were the assignment editor and this story were written for the NSU paper, what might you tell the reporter about the lead and organization?

Assignment 2. What additional reporting might you advise the reporter to do?

Assignment 3. Correct the grammar, style, wordiness and other errors in the story.

Northern State University's Denton Center for Creative Preschool Education has been well   1.

received by both faculty and students, Dr. Charlotte Myers, director of the center, said Tuesday dur-   2.

ing an open house marking the eighth anniversary of the school's opening.   3.

The school provides experimental education programs for 3 to 5 year olds and is funded by the   4.

university, the education department and the student government.   5.

"We are not just a daycare center," Dr. Myers said. "We are a center for development of sound   6.

education programs for preschool youngsters."   7.

She said the center's staff has been "exceedingly pleased" with the response to the school, located   8.

near the Northern State baseball complex.   9.

"When we opened, we had four fulltime teachers who had undergone a year of training, some   10.

professors in early education who were volunteering their time and 22 brave parents who enrolled 31   11.

children in an experimental program."   12.

Today the school has 18 teachers, 35 student teachers, scores of volunteers and 253 students. "As   13.

a matter of fact, we now have a waiting list to get into the school. Many faculty members enroll their   14.

children in our school before the children are even born," she said.   15.

Dr. Myers explained that many pregnant mothers come to the center and have their children's   16.

names placed on a waiting list for four years from now. "It's cute really," she said. "They use names   17.

like "Angel Williams" or "Baby Smith."   18.

Dorothy Franklin, who was at the open house and was obviously pregnant, said she had heard so   19.

much about the school she came to the open house to check it out. "I'm enrolling Junior today," she   20.

said patting her tummy.   21.

Franklin's friend, Sue Black, came to the open house with her. "Our children attended the school   22.

and they just loved it," Black said. "Bernie and Jen learned so much and developed such positive atti-   23.

tudes toward school and learning."   24.

Dr. Meyers said the center admits about 100 three-year-olds each fall. "We take 33 from the wait-   25.

ing list of faculty and staff, then 33 from the student waiting list," she said. "The remaining spots are   26.

filled on the basis of need like, say, a mother coming back to school or a new staff member with small   27.

children."   28.

Although the program is very popular, Myers said it is unlikely the program will grow.   29.

"In many ways we're too large now. We want to keep being an experimental program. It's hard to   30.

conduct good research when you have such a large facility." Meyers said that research done by NSU   31.

faculty at the Denton School has been published in both academic and trade publications. "Many of   32.

the programs being instituted by some of the nation's larger daycare centers were developed or tested   33.

here at Denton," she said.   34.

EXERCISE 56 NAME _____

Assignment 1. Identify the nut graf in this story.

Assignment 2. Edit the story for grammar, style, wordiness, conciseness, punctuation and so on.

Nicole Barton can't forget last shrill scream of her tiny Pomeranian.

Barton had taken her dog Poetess for their nightly stroll seven weeks ago when they were attacked by a pair of Bulldogs a block from her Northern City home

The two bulldogs charged out of a house on S. 9th St. Barton picked up her six year old dog to protect it. But the bulldogs leaped on Barton, knocking her done. Both dogs grabbed Poetess who was so severely injured that she needed to be euthanized.

Barton received a concussion and was treated at Northern City Hospital for bites and scratches on her arms and breasts.

"My body is healing," she said Tuesday. But the memories of the attack and the screams of the dog she had owned since it was puppy are still with her. I have trouble sleeping and I panic when I see a big dog. I don't think I could ever have another pet. My life is now miserable in so many ways."

Barton is now leading a fight against dangerous dogs. She wants County Commissioners to protect people from dangerous dogs by passing a zero-tolerance rule. The law would require any dog be muzzled and leashed in public after the first time it attacks without provocation.

"We can't continue to allow dangerous dogs to attack people on the street," Barton said. "If I had been carrying a baby instead of Poetess, they would have killed the child. People need to take responsibility for their dogs."

In the past, County officials had said that state law limits what local governments can do to regulate pets.

But Barton and her group Protect Everyone Today convinced Commission Ben Knight to ask county attorneys to find a way to increase regulations. County attorneys believe the proposed muzzle requirement will satisfy state regulations and still protects dogowners rights.

Current county laws requires owners of dogs deemed dangerous to be kept indoors or in a locked enclosure. But the process of getting a judge to rule that a dog is dangerous can take several days, and owners can appeal the judges decision to a county court.

"Right now I know of a case of a severely bitten child," Wilma Bowles, an attorney who has volunteered to help PET. "The vicious dogs are still roaming loose three months after the attack and animal control officers can't do a thing about it until those dogs attack again."

Knight's proposal requires any dog that has attacked a person or animal to be muzzled until a judge or court declares the dog safe. Dangerous dog proceedings also would begin immediately against any dog responsible for at least two such attacks.

"This is an urban environment with people living closer and closer together, and this would at least give us a way to eliminate repeat attacks by an animal," Knight said. "We're stricter with human criminals than we are with animal criminals. With this, everyone will realize there is a price to pay if their dog attacks."

More than 650 dog bites are reported each year to county animal control officers. The largest number of complaints of bites are filed against Pit Bulls, Rottweilers and German Shepherds.

Knight said the state legislature passed a measure ten years ago that prohibit county's from having laws against particular species of dogs.

Dr. Howard Colley, a northern City vet, said he will speak against the measure when it comes before the County commission.

"If this passes and they just muzzle the dogs, they are missing the boat," Colley said. "Muzzling will not give them the answer they are looking for. It's a behavioral problem that needs to be addressed. Muzzles only make dogs madder." He would require owners to take their dogs to pet training and obedience classes.

EXERCISE 57   NAME _____

Assignment 1. If you were an assignment editor, what might you say if you were coaching the writer of this feature? In particular, what might you say about its focus?

Assignment 2. Edit the feature for style, spelling, grammar and other errors.

The fog was thick in the air as Shazia Farhat walked gingerly through the Northern State University Arboretum, carefully scanning each leaf and eying every branch. It was her first time in the preserve on the east side of campus.

The 20-year-old biology student, glass bottle in hand, was searching for a buzzing bee or butterfly—the bugs would bring her extra lab credit and give her grade a needed boost.

"This is a quiet place—it looks like you're in the countryside," Farhat said. "You have all these beautiful things in here. I'm just scared about the snakes—I hope I don't find any."

NSU students and visitors have been exploring the arboretum since its inception in 1983, examining insects and studying native plants. The arboretum has undergone several changes and welcomed many visitors in its short life.

Most recently, the south end of the arboretum was intersected by construction of the Gemini Boulevard extension. Dr. Henry Whitman, director of the arboretum, says the project will not destroy the habitat. "Early on, some of the facilities planners told me we might have to move the arboretum because there would be a road passing through it, and I assured them that was no problem—roads pass through botanical gardens and arboreta all around the country, Whitman said.

"We've been heartily supportive of the (road extension) because even with 26,000 students on the campus now, with minor traffic problems, we can anticipate a great need for that road as we approach 40,000 students," Whitman said.

"The roadway has cut some trails and in future years, what we'll do is simply walk across the road and pick up the trail on the other side," he added.

Whitman, an avid ecologist, says the bottom line is that some sort of preserve survive for future study by students.

"Land on university campuses is almost beyond price," Whitman said. "It's easy enough to calculate the value of a piece of real estate in a urban neighborhood, but the value of an acre of land on a university campus is almost astronomical when you consider its possible applications.

"This is also why it becomes important to look to programs that will preserve appropriate pieces."

Dr. John Wise, an assistant professor in the biology department, is using the arboretum as his lab students study soil samples. "The NSU campus represents many areas of bio-diversity, as witnessed by the arboretum, Wise said. "And, it can provide a nice break from the library."

When NSU students aren't using the preserve as a real-world laboratory, community groups and international visitors are traversing the shaded trails.

In recent weeks, dignitaries from Russia and Japan toured the preserve. Local children from public schools as well as area garden club members also make regular visits.

Student and community volunteers tend the arboretum's plant displays and connecting paths. According to Whitman, more than 1,642 work hours were logged last year—more than 14,000 hours have been logged since 1986.

Arboreta are common on university campuses, according to Whitman. About 25 percent of the membership of the American Association of Botanical Gardens and Arboreta are college or university botanical gardens and arboreta.

Whitman hopes the arboretum remains a center of learning for students and visitors.

"I like to think that the arboretum would still be there (in years to come), still providing a representation of the different habitats that the area had to offer, but has more or less lost due to the very aggressive development in the region," Whitman said.

"That development is very necessary, but a the same time, we need to be able to protect selected areas for public recreation and education," Whitman added.

"When we lose that desire to learn about our environment, I think it's all over."

EXERCISE 58   NAME _____

Your campus newspaper is doing a package about spring break in Florida. The mainbar is about where to go and where to stay. The package includes the following two sidebars.

Assignment 1. If you were coaching the reporter, what suggestions might you make about the sidebars? Write them in the margins.

Assignment 2. Edit the sidebar for grammar, spelling, punctuation, word usage, accuracy and so on. Assume that names are spelled correctly on first reference.

TRADER BEACH, Fla –"Spring break sucks" is scrawled in soap on the back window of an aging Honda Civic that has just parked at a pulloff on Route A1A a few miles north of Trader Beach.

The driver and two passengers take their surfboards off of the top of the car and climb the wooden stairway over the sand dune and sea oats.

It's a cold March day by Floridas standards. They don black rubber wetsuits with irridescent stripes. The only skin left uncovered is their bronzed faces framed with sun-bleached hair.

It's not their favorite place to surf. The waves are small and the beach is rocky. But until spring breaking college students head back to classes in the North, this beach will have to do.

"We hate Spring Break," veteran surfer Dave Holden says later in a nearly-empty bar north of Trader Beach. He points to the corner pocket where he plans to sink the eight-ball. "The ocean gets too crowded and the breakers get in your way."

Holden and his two companions skipped work today. Early this morning, Holden dialed 675-SURF and heard a favorable surf report. They scraped together enough cash for gas, grub, and tolls and head out for Trader beach.

"If the waves are good, I'll always skip work," Holden said. "I just need to make enough money for my rent and a box of Captain Crunch."

Holden lives in a house in Bithlo, a small town about 20 miles from the Trader Beach, with Pat Iturrino and Tre Morris,

Holden is an ex-member of the Inland Ocean Surf Team of Orlando. Two years ago, he took second place in the Trader Beach Surf Tournament, one of the largest amateur contests on the East coast.

"We don't go much for competition anymore," Holden said. "Surfing is a stress reliever. There are no worries out there."

No worries? Their bodies tell another tale.

Iturrino has scares on his left arm from where a shark chewed on it. Morris has sea urchin spines lodged in the sole of his foot and walks with limp. Each surfer reported numerous stings from jellyfish and man-of-wars they have encountered over the years. Jellyfish are floating masses of goo that pack a potent sting that can prove fatal.

But the injuries rarely keep them from surfing.

After the shark attack, Iturrino received 50 stitches on his arm and spent two days in the hospital.

"Pat was surfing the day the stitches were removed," Holden said. "Did a good job too. Said he staid up on the board better because the salt water stung too much when he was in the water."

Iturrino's encounter with a shark is part of the price they pay to surf.

The surfers say they see the sharks all the time. Sometimes they come close, but they don't head for the shore.

"I'm not scared of them. I know I won't get bit again. It's just like lightning. Nobody gets bit twice," Iturrino said.

George Bobbins, 28, alias Ratstink, is the oldest member of the surf clan. With 20 years of surfing experience, Bobbins has come to respect the shark.

"I respect sharks. It's their territory we are invading," he said.

Parson seems to ponder Bobbins's comment. He takes a swig out of a beer and adds, "Yeah, it's our playground. It's their world."

Bobbins too has never let injuries keep him on dry land. He said he once did not busted his chin open on his surf board when a wave smashed him.

"The skin on his chin was flapping in the wind. I knew he needed stitches and I had the needle and thread to stitch it with," Iturrino joined in.

Robbins laid on the hood of his car and talked Iturrino into doing some surgery. As Robbins gulped and gritted his teeth, Iturrino sewed the wound shut with provisions from his first-aid kit. The surgery was a success and they went back to the beach.

"It hurt, but I wanted to surf some more, and I figured I'd save some money in doctor's fees," Heist said.

A ruptured eardrum couldn't stop Holden. Doctors told him to keep the ear dry. So he duck taped his ear shut and surfed anyway. In a follow-up visit, doctors said the hole in his eardrum had enlarged. Once again doctors gave Robins strict instructions to avoid the water.

"But the waves were outrageous one day, so I took a cotton ball and tied some fishing line around it. I put the cotton in my ear and sealed it in there with Superglue. It worked. It kept the water out. But it took me five days to get the cotton and string out,' Holden said. "I still hear ringing all the time."

Bobins said he lives for surfing. He calls it a gift from God.

"I wish more people could understand it. It's a natural high. All you need is a board and the natural energy surrounds you," he said.

EXERCISE 59   NAME _____

Here's the second sidebar in the spring break package.

Assignment 1. If you were coaching the reporter, what suggestions might you make about the sidebars? Write them in the margins.

Assignment 2. Edit the sidebar for grammar, spelling, punctuation, word usage, accuracy and so on. Assume that names are spelled correctly on first reference.

TRADER BEACH, Fla.—As it has for the past 10 years, Florida and its beaches tops the list as the most popular spring break destination for Northern State University students.

But one thing is different this year. Many of them say they aren't going into the water. They're afraid of sharks.

So far this year, the number of shark attacks are more than twice the average for Florida. Seven people have been bitten by sharks in just the past 19 days.

Shark attacks are nothing new in Florida. A scientific study found 79 confirmed, unprovoked attacks worldwide last year. Of those, 34 occurred in Florida. Fatalities are rare here, unlike in Austraila where a third of people attacked by sharks die.

The number of shark attacks are likely to be much higher this year. The combination of hungry sharks mingling with surfers and bathers will make that number grow, according to Connie Williams, head the Trader Beach beach patrol.

"That area has always had high concentration of bait fish. That draws sharks looking for food," Williams said. "The last couple of years, a slight warming of the water just off the beaches has attracked more bait fish right up to the shore. And the sharks are there with them."

She said that in 1988 the whole state had only 3 reports of people injured by sharks. Last year the Trader Beach area alone had three times that.

The frequency of attacks at trader beach in the past three weeks didn't surprise marine biologist Howard Davis of the Florida Museum of Natural History in Gainesville.

After digging into his records, Davis noted that the Trader Beech area has had the greatest number of shark bites on the east coast from the late 1880's through last Thursday. He concedes this year is particularly bad.

Davis said people shouldn't confuse Trader Beach sharks with great whites.

According to Davis, puppy sharks—young ones that really want to eat fish, not people, are the major threat in Trader Beach. They're bites are more scary than ferocious, Davis said. None of the bites have been fatal, and not many were even incapacitating.

He said sharks apparently do not find humans particularly tasty. Often they will approach a swimmer, recognize that it is a human and swim away. "That's why you hear so many people say they were "bumped" by a shark."

Davis said it was no mystery why the area had so many shark bites.

"The area has murky water which is perfect cover for sharks hunting fish and it has big waves which attract surfers. You put hungry sharks and playful surfers in the same shallow water, and somebody's going to get nibbled."

On Friday Eric Cohen, 19, a freshman at Eastern Indiana University received stitches for 3 and 4-inch cuts on his legs after an encounter with a shark. Fifteen minutes after Cohen was bitten four other surfers within 100 yards of Cohen reported being bumped by sharks. And two hours later, an unidentified surfer was bitten on his left foot, lifeguards said. The youth wrapped his wound in a towel and left the beach before authorities could take an official report.

Some Florida beeches are posting shark warnings. Signs along the beaches on popular Hutchinson Island near Ft. Pierce remind swimmers that they should leave the water immediately if a shark is cited nearby. According to the signs, it is a violation of a county ordinance not to report a shark citing immediately to life-guards. The sign doesn't say if it is a crime to falsely yell "Shark" on a crowded beech.

Despite all the publicity shark attacks get, Davis, the marine biologist, contends visitors to Floridas beechs have little to worry about.

"You're more likely to get hit by lightning while in Florida than you are to get biten by a shark," Davis says and then adds with smile, "of course Florida leads the nation in lightning strikes."

Connie Williams said the state has been passing out leaflets with these suggestions on how to avoid shark attacks:

1. Avoid swimming during at night, when sharks tend to be more active and feed

2. Stay together in groups when possible

3. Watch for situations where sharks are likely to be present, such as schooling fish or diving seabirds

4. Avoid places where sharks tend to congregate, such as areas between sand bars and the surf zones, or along edges of channels

5. Jewelry may look to a shark like sun reflecting off scales of a fish so don't wear any.

CHAPTER 8

HANDLING WIRE COPY

Newspapers buy news from the AP, Reuters and supplemental services owned by newspapers, news syndicates and chains.

Although wire copy has already been edited, don't assume that these stories will be free from error. They will need to be edited. Occasionally, wire editors will find factual problems and will call the services to get clarifications.

Editors often have to cut these stories—sometimes drastically. Before you cut information from a story, remove all the wordiness and repetition. You may be surprised at how much you can trim a story without removing any information or changing its tone.

Cut wisely. Don't automatically cut the color. Conciseness is a virtue. But you shouldn't make a lively story bland in the name of conciseness. And watch for "headless snakes." These are created when careless editors cut out the paragraph with the first reference to people and organizations but leave in a later reference to those people and organizations without their complete names or titles.

Often, wire editors rewrite stories completely so that they can be used in news roundups or as news briefs. Editors condense a full-length story to 100 words or so. This kind of condensation requires both good news judgment and well-honed writing skills.

Because many newspapers subscribe to more than one wire service, wire editors often take information from two or more wire stories and write a single story that better explains the news. They then credit these stories to the wire services. Because editors often lack time for a complete rewrite, they may pull sentences or whole paragraphs from each wire story as they piece together a new story. Then they add transitions and smooth out the writing to make the story flow well.

When editors find stories that have local angles, they usually send them to assignment editors, who give them to reporters to update. However, on small dailies or during busy times at larger papers, editors themselves rewrite the stories, localizing them.

EXERCISE 60   NAME _____

Practice exercise. Answers in back of book.

Assignment 1. Trim 30 words from this wire story. In the margins, explain why you made the changes. Make any needed corrections in AP style, grammar and spelling. Assume that Elwood is a city in your state. Compare yours with the edited version in the back of the book.

Assignment 2. Rewrite the story as an 80-word brief.

ELWOOD—Elwood police early Wednesday morning cited a train engineer after the train he was   1.

driving collided with a car and injured a Elwood woman at a crossing in downtown Elwood.   2.

It was the third time in two weeks that engineers have been ticketed by Elwood police at the same   3.

crossing.   4.

Lucille McKinney, 42, was driving her Buick across a double set of railroad tracks on State Road   5.

28 near Main Street when it was struck by a slow-moving Central Line engine.   6.

McKinney said she never saw the train coming. The engine' headlights were off, the railroad gates   7.

didn't come down, the warning lights didn't flash, and there was no flagman to warn cars that a train   8.

was coming, police said.   9.

The engineer, Lawrence Dillenger, 53, of Oakwood was cited for failing to use safety measures, a vio-   10.

lation of traffic laws. Dillenger told police he was not aware the lights on the train were not working.   11.

McKinney was taken by ambulance to University Hospital in Elwood, where she was treated for   12.

minor cuts and a broken leg. She was released later in the afternoon.   13.

Two weeks ago, police ticketed an engineer whose train sat in the crossing for 20 minutes, creat-   14.

ing traffic jams in Elwood's downtown area. Later that same day, police issued a speeding ticket to an   15.

engineer after the train he was driving passed through the crossing at 40 mph, 10 mph more than city   16.

ordinances allow.   17.

The crossing is at the entrance to a busy Central Line switching yard.   18.

EXERCISE 61   NAME _____

Assignment 1. Trim 40 words from this wire story. In the margin, explain why you made the changes.

Assignment 2. Make any needed corrections in AP style, spelling and so on. Assume that Brighton is a city in your state.

Assignment 3. Rewrite the story as a 100-word brief.

BRIGHTON—Knowing she would be gone only a couple of minutes, Dolores Effron left her 7-month-old granddaughter locked in car in Wednesday afternoon's 90-degree heat. When she returned, she discovered she had left her keys in the cars ignition.

Panicking, she called 911 and asked for help.

The dispatcher's response? There's nothing police can do.

The grandmother was told that police are no longer allowed to use special devices to unlock car doors. She should call a locksmith or AAA.

"I couldn't believe it," said an angry Dolores Effron.

"The dispatcher said the best she could do was to send a police officer out," Effron said. "But the officer couldn't help me. He could just stand there and watch me break a window or something and get Jody out of the car."

Effron's ordeal began when she left the infant in the car while she ran into a fast food restaurant on S. Main St. at about 2 p.m. Wednesday. "I had called-in my order like I do all the time. They already had it in a sack for me. I wasn't in the place more than 2 minutes." When she returned, she saw her keys still in the ignition of the locked car.

A few minutes after talking to the 911 operator, Effron flagged down a Logan County sheriff's deputy, and he called the Brighton Fire Rescue Department on his car radio.

Firefighters arrived a few minutes later to find Jody crying hysterically.

They used a special center punch to break the glass without hurting the baby. The tool causes glass to shatter downward instead of into the car's interior.

The baby's clothes were soaked with sweat when she was removed from the car. She was taken to University Hospital. Doctors treated her for dehydration and kept her overnight for observation.

"We were pretty lucky," Fire Rescue Captain Jose Martinez said. "On a hot day like Wednesday, if that baby had been in the car for, say, 10 minutes longer, it would have been a critical situation. Baby's bodies are small and they don't hold much water. Their cooling mechanism can be quickly overtaxed."

Police Chief Bruce Dodge said the 911 operator had not followed proper procedures. He said an officer should have been sent to the scene and determined what course of action should have been taken.

Dodge said he has ordered an investigation and placed the dispatcher, Suzanne Duncan, who has answered 911 calls for 5 years, on suspension.

"We handle calls like this everyday of the week," Dodge said. "We have locked cars and children are often in them. We always send officers out. I don't know what happened in this case."

Effron said she hopes Dodge is right. "I am interested that they do training and make sure that every operator knows what to do when a child is in jeopardy."

EXERCISE 62   NAME _____

Assume that you're working the wire desk at a small daily in Northern City. Fort Debbs is a larger city nearby. Because Fort Debbs is one of the cities mentioned in this wire story, you want to localize it. You check your paper's computerized morgue and find a recent story about the topic. Combine them into one story for the Northern City paper, editing also the mistakes in grammar and punctuation.

WASHINGTON—Sen. Marilyn Coates (Rep.Ky.) has called for a pause in the construction of seven Federal court houses, some of which Federal investigators likened to the Taj Mahal.

"Americans expect their courthouses to be enduring, solemn and majestic but there is a difference between stately and opulent," she said Friday night after a hearing.

The government may be spending too much on 'palatial accommodations' for Federal judges, she said.

The house passed a bill last mouth setting aside $900,000,000 for construction of the seven courthouses. However, senators slashed nearly $100,000,000 before passing the measure.

Coates, who heads the conference committee trying to iron out the differences in the bills, cited results of a study by the General Accounting Office, the investigative arm of congress.

The GOA found widely varying costs for the court houses, ranging from $31 million in Shreveport, La., to more than $400 million in New York City. The differences were due in part to varying materials, land values, and facilities. But, the GOA report said, some judges have 'cajoled architects into designing Taj Mahalls instead of public buildings.'

The GOA criticized what they called the 'excessively grand scale' of many of the buildings. They said the Boston courthouse will have hand-painted stenciling on the ceilings, costing about $700,000, and solid wood bookcases filled with law books behind each judges bench, even though 'most judges these days rely on computer databases not law books. They're there for show.'

The main lobby of the court house in Reno, Nev., will have granite walls and flooring that cost more than $800,000. The exterior walls of the New York building are granite, one of the most expensive materials available while the building in St. Louis has a costly highrise design featuring a split level lobby.

The report also questioned the size of the buildings. They said the Alexandria, Va., building had more court rooms and judges offices than were needed. They projected that some of the court rooms would remain unused for at least seventeen years.

The court houses are proposed for New York City, Boston, St. Louis, Shreveport, La., Reno, Nev., Alexandria, Va., Portland, Me. and Ft. Debbs.

You call the following story out of the newspaper's computerized morgue. It appeared in your paper last month.

FORT DEBBS—The Senate Tuesday gave the go-ahead to a $32 million dollar federal courthouse for downtown Fort Debbs.

Plans call for a three-story building on Main Street between Ninth Street and 10th Street. The present building, which was built in 1925, is so crowded that judges must share facilities. Court rooms are in use continually from 7:30 a.m. to 7 p.m.

The new building will provide each judge with a court room, chamber and library and house a number of federal agencies.

Architectural drawings indicate the building will have an exterior made of precast concrete and an entry patio covered by bronzed glass.

Rep. James Cohen, R-Fort Debbs, who headed the drive in Congress for the court house, said the building is large enough to accomodate the growth in the area.

"We wanted to make sure we build a courthouse that would serve the needs of this district for at least 50 years," he said. "It will be a nice addition to downtown Fort Dodds"

Andrea Porter, President of the Spring County Bar Assn. said they were elated that the building won approval. "We've worked hard to bring this about. The present building outlived its usefulness year's ago."

No date has been set for construction.

CHAPTER 9

MATH AND THE JOURNALIST

AVERAGE CAN MEAN MANY THINGS

In everyday life, you probably use the notion of "average" in at least three ways. Mathematicians have names for them:

Mean is the average you are using when you figure your grade in a class. To get the mean, you add up your test scores and divide by the number of tests.

Median is the number in the middle of the list. Half the numbers are higher than the median and half are lower. When you describe an athlete as average, you are probably using this notion of average. Many players are better; many are worse.

Mode is the most common number in the list. If you're pooling money to buy a friend a present, you might ask how much other people are giving. You might then give what seems to be the most common amount. To mathematicians, you've decided to give the mode.

CALCULATING INCREASES AND DECREASES

Often, stories report that pilots want 10 percent raises or that the university budget has been cut by 18 percent. Here's how to figure how much money is involved:

If your salary is going up 5 percent and you make $10 an hour now, how much will you make in the future? Turn 5 percent into a decimal: 5 percent as a decimal is .05. Multiply your current salary ($10) by .05. You get .50. Your salary will go up 50 cents to $10.50 an hour.

If your salary is going down 5 percent, turn 5 percent into the decimal .05 and then multiply. $10 an hour times .05 equals .50. Your salary is going down $.50 and you will earn $9.50.

FIGURING PERCENTAGE OF INCREASE OR DECREASE

Reporters often want to put numbers in context by saying that the new budget is 5 percent higher than the old one or that crime is 10 percent lower this year than last. The procedure to determine this percentage is to subtract the smaller number from the larger number and divide the result by the old number. Here are some examples:

You were making $10 an hour. Your salary is raised to $11. What percentage is your increase? Subtract the smaller number from the larger one. $11 minus $10 equals $1. Divide the result by the old number ($10): 1 divided by 10 equals .10. Turn that into a percent by multiplying by 100: 100 times .10 equals 10. You got a 10 percent raise.

You were making $10 an hour, but business is slow. Your salary is cut to $9.50. What percentage did your salary decrease? Subtract the smaller number ($9.50) from the larger number ($10). You get $.50. Divide $.50 by the older salary ($10). You get .05. To change that to a percent, multiply by 100: 100 times .05 equals 5 percent. Your pay was cut 5 percent.

Sales tax in your state is going up. It was 6 percent. It will soon be 8 percent. What is the percentage of increase? The temptation is to subtract 6 from 8 and say that taxes will be going up 2 percent. But that's not accurate. You are actually subtracting 6 percentage points from 8 percentage points, and the result is 2 percentage points. You could report that sales tax is going up 2 percentage points. But you probably want to report the percentage of increase. You figure it just as you did the percentage of increase in the salary example, like this:

Subtract the smaller number (6) from the larger number (8). You get 2. Divide 2 by the old number (6): 2 divided by 6 is .33. Multiply by 100 to turn that into a percent. The sales tax will go up 33 percent.

Imagine that the state decides to lower the sales tax from 8 percent to 6 percent. To determine the percentage of decrease, subtract the smaller number (6) from the larger (8). You get 2. Divide 2 by the old number (8): 2 divided by 8 is .25. The sales tax is going down 25 percent.

FIGURING PERCENTAGE LARGER OR SMALLER

Women earn 10 percent less than men. Boys score 8 percent higher on math tests than girls. Here's how you figure percentages larger or smaller. The procedure is to subtract the numbers to get the difference and then divide by the target salary, like this:

Suppose that Jim makes $15 an hour and Beth makes $20. Subtract the smaller number from the larger to get the difference. It's $5. If you want to know how much higher Beth's salary is than Jim's, divide the difference ($5) by Jim's salary ($15). 5 divided by 15 is .33. To turn that into a percent, multiply by 100: .33 times 100 equals 33 percent. You could say that Beth makes 33 percent more than Jim.

If you want to know how much less Jim makes than Beth, divide the difference in their salaries ($5) by Beth's salary ($20). 5 divided by 20 is .25 or 25 percent. Jim earns 25 percent less than Beth.

FIGURING RATES

Often, statistics are more understandable if you compare them on a per capita basis. The murder rate is 12 per 100,000 in one city and 24 per 100,000 in another. The procedure to figure rates is to divide the number of events by the total population. To determine the rate per 1,000, multiply the result by 1,000. For rate per 10,000, multiply by 10,000.

Suppose that there were 70 muggings in a city of 8,000 residents. Divide 70 by 8,000 and you get 0.00875. Multiply the result by 1,000 and you can 8.75. You can report that the city has 8.75 muggings per 1,000 residents. Multiply the result by 10,000 and you get 87.5. You can report that the city has 87.5 muggings per 10,000 residents.

EXERCISE 63

Practice exercise. Answers in back of book.

1. The state gave grants to several schools in your community. Here's the listing:

School	Amount	School	Amount
Southside	$1,000	Roosevelt	$8,000
Lincoln	$12,000	Reagan	$3,000
Jefferson	$1,000	Adams	$1,000
Spock	$3,000	Washington	$8,000
North	$5,000	Monroe	$1,000

   What were the mean, medium and mode of the grants?
2. The paper says it will hire 12 new reporters. There are 80 people in the newsroom now. The number of journalists in the newsroom will go up how much percent?
3. The newspaper you work for has just announced that everyone is getting a 5 percent raise. You make $25,000 now. What will your new salary be?
4. The state announced that state income tax will go from 2 percent a year to 3 percent.
   a. State income tax is going up how much percent?
   b. State income tax is going up how many percentage points?
5. The county school superintendent believes the county has a real problem with pregnancy among high school students. He releases these figures comparing your county with a neighboring county.

	Girls in high schools	Pregnancies
Your county	7,500	390
Neighboring county	6,100	230

   What is the pregnancy rate per 1,000 girls in each county? (Round to the nearest whole number.)
6. Your reporter discovers that the average high school pregnancy rate is about 45 per 1,000. Marshall County has a rate of 60 per 1,000. Marshall County is ___ percent higher than the national average.
7. The schools in Marshall County started an education campaign. The high school pregnancy rate has dropped from 60 per 1,000 to 45 per 1,000. You could write, "High school pregnancy rate has dropped ____ percent in Marshall County."
8. Your paper does a poll. In the race for governor, Jimenez has 42 percent, Morgenstern has 40 percent and Williams has 15 percent. The margin of error is 3 percent. Your political reporter has written a story saying Jimenez leads and Williams is a distant third. What changes in the story might a statistically minded copy editor suggest?
9. A week later, Morgenstern is endorsed by the current governor, who is very popular. The new poll has these numbers: Morgenstern, 43 percent; Jimenez, 41 percent; and Williams, 16 percent. Your political reporter writes a story about how much the endorsement has helped Morgenstern. What changes in the story might a statistically minded copy editor suggest?
10. Your political reporter listens to the statistically minded copy editor's suggestions. "The problem," the reporter concludes, "is in the margin of error." He suggests that the newspaper should hire better pollsters so that the margin of error won't be so high. What does the copy editor say to that?

EXERCISE 64   NAME _____

1. Sanford last year had 325 burglaries and Cicero had 643. Sanford has a population of 72,000; Cicero, 120,000. How many burglaries per 1,000 residents did each city have?

2. The school has a new reading test for fifth-graders. Here are the results:

	Passed	Failed
Girls	745	23
Boys	702	53

What percentage of boys passed the test?

What percentage of girls passed the test?

3. The mayor wants her salary raised to $50,000. The state average for a city the size of yours is $40,000. You could report: "If the mayor gets the new pay raise, she will be earning ____ percent more than the state average."

4. The police chief now makes $40,000. The mayor wants to increase his salary to $44,000. You could write, "The police chief will receive a _____ percent raise."

5. During his campaign, the sheriff says he has hired more officers and increased their average pay. Here's the data:

Rank of officer	Last year number	Last year salary	This year number	This year salary
Deputy chiefs	3	$50,000	3	$75,000
Captains	9	$40,000	10	$60,000
Investigators	20	$35,000	20	$35,000
Patrolmen	100	$25,000	120	$25,000

a. Has the sheriff hired more officers? What's the percentage of increase?

b. What were the mean, median and mode salaries last year?

c. What were the mean, median and mode salaries this year?

d. Which of these "averages" has the most meaning in this example?

6. Governor Jones has announced a plan for state income tax cuts. Corporations now pay 10 percent of their income. Individuals pay 15 percent. The governor's plan reduces corporate taxes to 5 percent and individual taxes to 10 percent.

a. If you were the PR person for the government, how might you—honestly and mathematically correctly—describe the tax cuts as being equal? Be careful with your wording.

b. How might someone—honestly and mathematically correctly—disagree and say the governor's cuts favor one side? Be careful with your wording.

If you were editing a story about the cuts, which of these descriptions (the one in answer A or the one in answer B) would be the most accurate way of reporting the tax cuts?

7. Monday, pollsters said that candidate Jones had 42 percent of the vote, Wilson had 40 percent and the rest of the voters were undecided, with a margin of error of plus/minus 3 points. Tuesday, Jones makes a homophobic remark to a heckler. A poll Wednesday finds that Jones has dropped to 40 and Wilson is now ahead with 42 percent with the rest of the voters undecided. The reporter writes a story saying that the homophobic remark has hurt Jones' reputation and he is no longer in first place. What would you say to the reporter if you were the editor?

8. Jones said he was not going to apologize to your city's gay population. The newest poll shows Jones at 35 percent, Wilson at 40 percent and the rest undecided. How might you describe what's happening in the race?

EXERCISE 65   NAME _____

Edit these stories for style, grammar, punctuation and so on. Pay particular attention to the use of numbers. Write any questions you would ask the reporter about these stories.

STORY 1

A 17 year old driver has been charged with 27 traffic violations after he and four friends led Northern City police on a high speed chase Tuesday night.

The chase begun when Officer Patricia Bowles tired to stop a car driven by Lee James on Main St. near the Northern City Mall.

The car, a Porsche Boxster, sped away. Bowles police cruiser was not able to stay with the car.

But Cicero County sheriff's deputy spotted the car traveling at least 80 miles per hour down Southern Ave. Soon more than 20 officers from the NCPD, the sheriff's department and the state police joined in.

After a 15 minute chase, Lee surrendered when he drove over metal stripes police placed on Maple Drive. The strips contain spikes that flattened two of Lee's tires causing the car to spin out of control.

Crammed into the two seat sports car were Lee, 231 South Brook Lane, Martha Morse, 17, 1932 North Tenth Street, Jorge Maunez, 18, 1643 Oakdale Avenue and Debbie Pratt, 19, 423 West Ninth Street.

Lee was charged with 12 counts of running stop signs, 8 counts of speeding, 1 count of fleeing police, 5 counts of illegal lane changes and 4 counts of traveling the wrong way on a one way street.

STORY 2

After a heated discussion Tuesday night, the Northern City Council decided to increase property taxes of both businesses and homes by two percent.

"We decided that raising them both the same was the only fair thing to do," said Council member Sue Quartos.

Larry Bibby argued that the council should raise business taxes more. "Home-owners have to pay too much now. Businesses are in better shape to be taxed.

Taxes for businesses will go from one percent to three percent. Homes will be taxed at six percent instead of the current four percent.

STORY 3

Mayor Julio Martinez's reelection campaign received a major boost when he was endorsed by popular Governor Jack Gilliam endorsed him.

Martinez now leads challenger Tova Jansson in polls done by the Dwight and Jones Polling firm.

Gilliam called Martinez one of the most effective mayors in the state and praised him for the city's growth in high tech industries.

Martinez had 53 percent of the vote last week. In a poll down immediately after the Governor's announcement, his lead jumped to 56 percent. Jansson's support dropped from 40 percent to 38 percent. Many Northern City voters are undecided.

CHAPTER 10

WRITING HEADLINES

Headlines should help attract readers to stories. Never settle for a dull headline just because it fits the space allotted. Make the extra effort to create headlines that are as appealing as possible.

Read and understand the story as you edit it. Make sure that you understand the elements of the story that make it important, interesting or different. Also watch for any needed qualifiers that must be included in the headline. If the person has been charged with a crime, the headline should not find the person guilty.

Write a rough headline, experimenting with word combinations that will form one or more lines of the headline. Try to find word groupings that suit the story and are interesting. You can then build those groupings into a first-class head. Don't worry so much about getting the head to fit at this point. Try to create the best possible head that's roughly the right size. If your headline is weak at this stage, it will probably get even weaker when you try to make it fit.

Choose specific, precise words and make every word count. Headlines that tell the news are usually better than vague ones. You are trying to find ways to attract readers to the story. The more angles you can put in your headlines, the more likely you are to attract readers. Don't stick words into your headline just to fill out the headline:

Use action verbs—and some creativity. There are lots of ways to write dull heads. Weak and passive verbs are frequent villains. Try to pick verbs that create images in the readers' minds. Use a dictionary or thesaurus. And if it would be appropriate for the story, consider word plays or puns that might interest readers and help them understand the story.

Start over if you're stuck. Lots of times, copy editors have great ideas for headlines. Unfortunately, those great heads sometimes don't fit the space. As painful as it may be, you have to forget the really great headline and go back to the beginning.

Headline orders tell the copy editor what size headline to write. Headlines have to fit a certain space on the page, so the copy editor must write a headline that fits. Usually, the people who design pages decide what kind of headlines the stories will receive. Traditionally, they have given headline orders that look like this:

35-36-2

That tells the copy editor that the headline will be 35 picas wide. The type size will be 36 points. And there will be two lines.

COUNTING HEADLINES

Before computers entered the newsroom, editors had to count the letters in their headlines to make sure that they would fit the space. They might have to write a headline with 14 letters in each line. Obviously, large letters such as *W* take up more space than small letters such as *i*. So editors used what some called the flirt system, because the small letters spelled out the word *flirt*. These small letters counted ½. Here's the complete system:

- The number 1; the letters *f, l, i, r, t*; capital *I*; *j* in some fonts, and most punctuation count ½.
- Most lower-case letters count 1.
- Most capital letters, lowercase *m* and *w,* and numbers except *1* count 1½.
- Capital *M* and *W* count 2.
- Spaces can count either a half or 1.

/ / /　　　　 /　　 /　　 /　　　　 /　　　 /

Morris decides to leave Senate

// / / / / / /　// // // / / / / / / / / /　/　/

Some editors drew little lines under the letter for each whole count and a line above a letter for a half count. They could then quickly count the little lines and find that this head counted about 28.

Editors were given charts, called headline schedules, which told them how many counts *each line* of a head should have. The charts varied by font, but here's one you can use for these exercises. The width of the headline is in the left column and the point size is across the top. A 48-point headline that is 78 picas wide will count 33.

Table 10.1. HEADLINE SCHEDULE

	14pt	18pt	24pt	30pt	36pt	42pt	48pt	60pt	72pt
11p (1 col)	26	18	14	11	9	8	5		
23p (2 col)	55	41	31	24	20	16	13	8	6
35p (3 col)	84	63	47	37	31	25	21	18	12
47p (4 col)		85	63	51	42	33	28	22	20
59p (5 col)		99	74	60	50	38	32	26	24
71p (6 col)		106	79	64	53	39	33	30	27

CHAPTER **11**

LIBEL AND FAIRNESS

Truth is a defense in libel cases in most states. Ultimately, reporters are responsible for the truthfulness of stories. But editors can head off some factual problems by asking these questions:

- Do the credentials of the sources seem appropriate? A police reporter once quoted a police officer as saying the victim had only minor injuries. The victim died in the hospital that night of major internal injuries. The lesson: Police officers are not the best sources for medical opinions.
- Has the reporter contacted a variety of sources? For example, if a story about problems in the university's financial aid office has only students as sources, editors will ask for more reporting. A truer picture of events, people or programs usually emerges when readers are given several perspectives.
- Is the story internally consistent? If facts or implications in one part of the story differ from those in another, good editors grow suspicious.

Another defense is privilege, meaning that the material is taken from court documents or from official proceedings of governmental bodies. Stories based on these documents are usually libel-proof unless the reporting is inaccurate or unfair.

A third defense comes from the Supreme Court's ruling in *Times v. Sullivan,* which affords newspapers greater protection when dealing with public figures. For public figures to win suits, they must show that journalists either knew the information was false before they printed it or were exceedingly reckless in the way they gathered the information. These standards are designed to allow the media to investigate the activities of government without fear that honest mistakes might result in costly libel suits. However, reporters and editors should not use this extra latitude to justify careless reporting.

Being fair is a constant challenge to journalists, and much of that burden falls to editors. Here are some guidelines to keep in mind:

- Avoid stereotypes. They're easy but unjustifiable ways to develop a story. Similarly, don't expect one person to speak for all members of diverse groups. For example, don't give the impression that one or two female professors' experiences represent those of all women in academia.
- Mention a person's race and gender only when it's necessary. Also try to ensure that stories represent the diversity in the community.
- Present all sides of the story, especially the views and reactions of people or organizations who have been attacked.
- Avoid saccharin and "gee whiz" tones in stories about the accomplishments of people who overcome societal or physical challenges, such as women, minorities or wheelchair-bound people.
- Treat people in the news, especially those drawn into the day's events by circumstance, the way you would want the media to treat members of your own family.

EXERCISE 66   NAME _____

Practice exercise. Answers in back of book.

Assignment 1. If you were the assignment editor, what comments might you make to the reporter about the fairness and accuracy of this story? What specific advice would you give?

Assignment 2. Edit the story for grammar, style, awkwardness and so on. Assume that it's for a small daily in Northern City, where NSU is. An edited version is in the back of the book.

African-American students will pause Monday to remember Martin Luther King, a civil rights leader who founded the National Assn. for the Advancement of Colored People.

Classes and university offices will be closed for the day.

Tricia Blair, president of the African-American Student Union, said an inter-faith prayer ceremony will be held on the quadrangle in front of the university's administration building. Among the clergy who have agreed to attend are the Rev. Carl Weaver of the Baptist Student Union, Father Wiley O'Roarke of St. Mary's Catholic Church, Rabbi Seymour Horst of Beth Israel, Imam Mohammed Ali of the Northern City Moslem church, and Grant Viceroy of the Black Muslims.

The NSU library has a special display about King's life. He was assassinated in Memphis, Tenn., in 1986.

EXERCISE 67   NAME _____

Assignment 1. If you were the assignment editor, what comments might you make to reporters about the fairness of these stories? What specific advice would you give them?

Assignment 2. Edit the stories for grammar, style, awkwardness and so on. Assume that they're for a small daily in Northern City, where NSU is, and that Springdale is a nearby city.

STORY 1

Police Tuesday night charged a 35-year-old mother with distributing child pornography, including pictures of her own teen-aged daughters and several of their friends from Southview Middle School engaged in sex acts with adult men.

Doris Slocum, 3265 W. 32nd Avenue, was taken into custody after police found hundreds of pictures of young girls stored in her computer.

Sgt. Jackie Gray said police had received a tip that Slocum was operating an Internet site, called Young Lovers. For a fee, users of the site could download the pictures into their own computers.

STORY 2

A man with three small sons was robbed by a black man Tuesday night as they were leaving a basketball game at Northern State University's Barr Arena.

Charles Nelson, 31, 321 S. East Street, told police that a man demanded that he hand over his wallet. When Nelson hesitated, the gunman pulled out a gun and aimed it at Nelson's 8 year old son Justin and threatened to kill Jamie, 6, and Jerome, 5.

After Nelson gave him his wallet, the gunman ordered Nelson and his sons to lay on the ground and told them to count to 10. He then ran from the parking lot.

Nelson said the man was wearing blue jeans and a dark hooded suit shirt with a scarf over his face. He could not give police a description of the robber's face, but he said he was black, medium build and athletic.

Police later took a man into custody. According to witnesses, they questioned Xavier Williams outside the arena and then took him to police headquarters. Police records indicate that Xavier, 18, 5412 Brook Ridge Apts., was later released and police gave him a ride home. Witness said his clothing and general description matched the robbers.

STORY 3

A former meat cutter at a Northern Starlight Food Store said he plans to file a class action lawsuit against the food chain accusing it of selling tainted meat.

"We were told to take old meat, soak it in Clorox bleach, douse it in barbeque sauce and turn it over to the deli," Bob Gross, 41, told reporters at a press conference in his home. "If it was too bad for the deli, we'd grind it up with some fresh meat and sell it as hamburger. I'd never eat anything from Northern Starlight myself."

Gross said he hopes a class action suit will stop the practice and get refunds for people who may have purchased spoiled meat. "I'm sure lots of people have gotten sick eating the meat I was forced to sell, and that hangs heavy on my conscience," he said.

He says his attorney will file the suit as soon as the labor relations board settles his complaint charging Northern Starlight dismissed him unfairly.

EXERCISE 68   NAME _____

Assignment 1. If you were the assignment editor, what comments might you make to reporters about these briefs? What specific advice would you give them?

Assignment 2. Correct any errors you find in grammar, style, spelling, wordiness and so on. Assume that the briefs are for a small daily in Northern City and that Springdale is a nearby city.

STORY 1

A would-be mugger Tuesday night learned to pick on people his own size.

The 5-foot-6, 140-pound young man targeted Denise Brunberger, 32, and Gloria Whitbread, 29, who live in West Wind Apartments as they were leaving a weight-control class in the basement of the First Baptist Church on West Jefferson St.

As the thief grabbed Brunberger's purse, he tripped, twisted his ankle and fell to the ground. Immediately, Brunberger saw her opportunity.

She threw her body on top of the youth and held him down while Whitbread ran to call police. Police reports describe her as being about 5-foot-4 and weighing 360-pounds.

The young man began moaning in pain and shouting for help. But even after a crowd of spectators encircled them, Brunberger continued to sit on him and bounce if he made efforts to escape until police arrived approximately 10 minutes later.

"She had him covered so completely we didn't even see him under her at first," one police officer remarked. "This is one time the crook was happier to see us than his intended victim was."

Jason DeSalvo, 18, 231 S. 6th St., was charged with theft and assault and battery. He was taken to Northern City Hospital where he was treated for a broken ankle and two broken ribs.

STORY 2

To Kurt Wheeler, Halloween night provided the perfect cover for crime.

The 19-year-old entered the Burger Island restaurant on S. 15th St. wearing a Woody Woodpecker costume. He stood patiently in line. Then, when it was his turn to order, he pointed a gun at the clerk and demanded all the money from his till. Wheeler put the money in a Burger Island sack and walked out.

Joseph Iago, the counterman, could not give detectives a description of Wheeler. "I couldn't see any of him," Iago said. "That bird costume covered him from head to toe, or beak to claw."

Detectives found the costume stuffed into a trash can behind the restaurant.

Later in the evening, they arrested Wheeler at his home. Police said they recognized Wheeler's modus operandi. He had committed a similar armed robbery last Halloween at a Dixie's Best Fried Chicken shop two blocks from the Burger Island restaurant. Charges were latter dropped in that crime.

Wheeler is being held in the county jail on suspicion of armed robbery.

STORY 3

Harriet Brunson and Gertrude Rosenstein weren't suspicious when they received phone calls from a local clinic saying that technicians had forgotten to perform one procedure in their recent mammogram.

The young man said the error was his fault, he apologized profusely and then offered to come to their homes to perform the final test. Because the caller knew so much about the treatment that they had received at Lakeview Medical Clinic, the women believed he must be on the clinic staff.

A few minutes later, the women said, a young man wearing a green medical uniform came to their homes. They said the man asked them to disrobe and then "examined" their bodies with his hands for he called "venial polyps that may indicate the presence of cancer." He then took several pictures of various parts of their bodies using a camera he said contained "special x ray film."

"He was a nice young man, very polite," Brunson, 61, 22A Brookside Apts., told police detectives later. "I thought sure he was from the doctors office. He said he would really feel bad if I got cancer because of his mistake."

Her neighbor, Gertrude Rosenstein, 69, 19B Brookside Apts., told her that a similar thing had happened to her the previous week at the same clinic and that the same man had come to her home to do the tests.

Brunson thought nothing more of the incident until she visited her doctor a couple of months later and mentioned how helpful the technician had been. The doctor told her he knew of no such tests.

Brunson and Rosenstein were shown photographs of all employees of the clinic. They said none of them were the man who came to their homes. Police are trying to determine how access to the clinic's medical records was obtained.

"We're dealing with a creep who took advantage of two old widows who live alone and are extremely gullible," police Sgt. Mike Murphy said.

CHAPTER **12**

PUTTING IT ALL TOGETHER

In this section, you will be given stories to edit.

1. Correct the grammar, spelling, punctuation and AP Stylebook errors.
2. Assume that names are correct on first reference.
3. Write headlines as assigned by your instructor.

EXERCISE 69   NAME _____

The City Council decided Monday night, to stop restaurants from serving alcohol in side walk cafes. 18 restaurants will have two weeks to close their outdoor facilities.

Mariam Ipollito, executive director of the Alliance for Drug Free Youth gave a ninety minute speech during which she tried to convince the council to change the law. She said she was concerned that allowing alcohol in the public right-of-way could cause problems such as drunken driving and under-age drinking. She said she had seen people in the side walk cafes toss bottles of beer to teen's driving by the cafes.

Some council members agreed.

"I understand the pleasure that comes with having a drink in dining areas on the side walk," said Mayor Christy Suzuki. "But I also understand the enforcement issues that come with that. It's getting too rowdy." The Mayor said police often find drunken students laying in the streets downtown.

Sylvia Tetherbaum, owner of Silly Syl's bar on Second Street said downtown was deserted after 5:00 p.m. until about eight years ago. Then bar owners began to buy portions of a decaying warehouse district and open their establishments. Now, a group of businesses are busy everynight, she said.

"We've got a real night-life now downtown," Syl said. "It's cool to be downtown. If you destroy this, you will be hurting the city and it's culture." She said the sidewalk bars and outdoor dining was the most profitable part of her bars business. "You take that away from me and I guarantee you that Silly Syl's is history.

Although council members said they recognized the role of outdoor dining in making downtown vibrant and more appealing, several expressed reservations about taking a portion of the sidewalks away from the public.

Councilman Dennis Holz pointed out that the city had just spent $5,200,000 dollars to improve the downtown area. Side walks were widened and re-surfaced.

"Today those side walks are roped off for the outdoor cafes," said Councilman Holz. Once we let them fence areas off, the public can't use them." He added that the city needs the whole sidewalk when hosting street fairs and other public events.

Two restaurants will not be effected by the law. Mahoney's, 231 South Maple Avenue and The Italian Kitchen, 328 East Main Street, will be grandfathered in. Each of them have had outdoor beer and wine gardens since prohibition was repealed in the 1930's. If these restaurants move or change owners, they will lose their exemption.

The Council has been debating the issue for 2 months. Presently the city has conflicting laws. A law passed eight years ago allowed the sale of special alcohol permits to establishments with sidewalk cafes. This summer, the Alliance for Drug-Free Youth filed a complaint against the city after their attorney discovered a 1951 city law that banned drinking on city owned property. The side walks are owned by the city.

EXERCISE 70   NAME _____

Jenny Dutton is sketching pictures of her classmates. Sitting next to her at Patrick Henry Middle School, Kyle Vivinetto draws racing cars. Haydee Gutierrez is building a house with plastic blockes. All the while, Teacher Robyn Leach walks around encouraging the students.

And this is math class.

Her teacher says that when Jenny can write and draw as part of a lesson, she gets more excited about what she's learning.

"Bookwork is boring," said Jenny, 13, a seventh-grader. "Fortunately, we're doing a lot more projects this year."

Leach says that Haydee and Kyle need to visualize what they are being taught.

Leach and other teachers at Patrick Henry in Elmwood have been schooled in a new educational theory. They have been taught to encourage the artistic eagerness that is common with middle school aged students.

The training is based on the teachings of Harvard Psychologist Howard Gardner. He believes that students have eight basic learning styles, such as linguistic, musical, kinesthetic and naturalist.

Professor Gardner thinks human beings learn in different ways and should not be judged according to a single standard, such as an IQ test. He wants teachers to present each lesson in several styles, such as using writing, music, experiments and group activities. He says students will learn the material better because they will be comfortable with at least one of the styles.

For her American Geography class, Social Studies Teacher, Shane Beasley, asked the students to create postcards from various areas of the country. He said it hit at least three of the learning styles: verbal-linguistic (writing the card), visual-spatial (designing it) and intra-personal (working by themselves).

"It's great," Shane said. "Everyone got real excited. Kids had to find out about the states and where things like the Grand Canyon and the Mt. Rushmore were." For another assignment, students worked in groups to build models of the St. Louis Arch and Devils Tower in Arizona.

"This is good for both the teacher and the students," Shanon said. We judge kids by more than just test scores. Allot of us don't test well." But, Shanon said, this program lets them show creativity and originality in addition to test scores.

Gardner's theory is in use at several schools throughout the nation. Followup studies have found that schools using the system have improved test scores as well as less absenteeism and more parental involvement.

Frustrated by administrators' emphasis on testing, the new approach has been embraced by many educators. They believe it shows children learn and demonstrate their understanding in a variety of ways.

"Adults usually have a single intelligence they are most comfortable with," said Marilyn Goldstein, priniple of Patrick Henry. "They like to talk or they like to write or they like to listen to music, and do best when they communicate in that style".

But she said children experiment with different styles, so teachers are encouraged not just to teach to their strengths but to expose them to a variety of ways to learn, she said.

Money to train teachers in the technics came from a grant from a state program to improve special education in the middle schools.

EXERCISE 71   NAME _____

A police are looking for a low-key con man that has been posing as a Cicero County Sheriff's deputy and conning convenience store clerks into cashing phony paychecks for him.

In each instance, the scam was slightly different but the end result was the same: the unidentified man walked out with nearly $500 in cash each time.

On April 7th, the man handed a clerk at a Cumberland Farm store in Michigan St. a note that he said was written by the store's manager. The note said it was OK to cash the mans paycheck, said Detective Tom Morgan.

When the clerk refused, the conman asked him to keep the note and ask the manager about it later. The clerk told Morgan, "The guy wasn't mad or anything. He said he understood and ask me if I'd keep the note. I said sure and put it by the cash register."

A few hours later, the man returned to the store and asked another clerk to cash his check. He told the clerk that the manager had left a note saying it was OK.

The 19-year-old clerk found the note beside the register. But there was not enough cash in the till to cover the check. He told the man to come back a few hours later. The man did, and the clerk handed over $562, Morgan said.

At a 7-11 store, the clerk told the man that the clerks were not allowed to cash checks. The man came back a few minutes later and told the clerk that he had talked with the manager, who agreed to cash the $498 paycheck, minus an $8 handling fee and $9 that the suspect's mother supposedly owed the store.

"I guess I figured he must be on the level or he would have wanted all the money," the clerk told police. "Besides, he was a police officer and I know how hard it is to cash a big check at night."

The clerk saw the same man at a gas station on April 20th, wrote down his license plate number and called police, but it turns out the vehicle, a black Ford Ranger, was stolen the day before.

The man has pulled off at least two other scams within the past month, one at a gas station on West Colonial Drive and one at a small food store in South 7th Ave., Morgan said.

The man identifies himself as Derrick Lewis. Witnesses say he is wearing what appears to be an authentic police uniform. Police emphasis that he is not employed by the Sheriff's Office.

The checks are phony, too. They are the type that can be bought at an office supply store. Morgan said the man fills in all of the information with a typewriter.

EXERCISE 72   NAME _____

Every student's dreams may have come true at Lincoln High School—for a short time any way.

School officials acknowledged Tuesday that two students had hacked their way into the school's computer and were changing classmate's grades for five dollars.

Now diplomas and college entrance paperwork is being delayed while teachers reexamine all the grades of the 2,500 students at the school.

Two students, described as "computer whizzes," have been accused of violating the student code that forbids "illegal or unethical use of school computers," officials said.

School officials said official grade transcripts will not include grades from this year until all grades have been checked by teachers. This may be a hard ship for college bound seniors. They must provide up to date transcripts to universities they would like to attend.

Graduation may be delayed if the grade checks are not completed in time according to school officials.

"This is a serious matter, and it must be dealt with seriously," a school district spokesman said.

One suspect's parents said their son was being accused of 'completely-bogus' charges. Parents of the other boy said there son only provided computer help to friends, and but did not change grades himself.

School officials would not release the boys names because they are 14 years old.

This papers policy is to not name minors accused of serious crimes unless they are tried in adult court rather than in the juvenile justice system.

District investigators are trying to determine whether other students were involved, said Joe Melita, executive director of the district's investigative unit.

No one knows how many records were changed, but at least twenty student have admitted to paying $5 to have their grades changed, Assistant Principal Patricia Browne said.

But all teachers were asked in a memo Tuesday to 'review your grades in previously saved documents'.

Two years ago, Lincoln High became a test facility for a centralized computer system called the e-gradebook. Every grade, including test and quiz scores, are entered into the system by teachers. The system is designed to provide guidance councilors and other school administrators with up to date information on students progress.

When the system was installed, representatives of Associated Educational Software boosted that the system was "the most secure system outside of the Pentagon." They said a combination of firewalls and passwords made it all but impossible to hack.

One student who asked to remain anonymous said that many students considered the statement a challenge. "Guys at the Computer Club said they could get in," he said. "They said it would take a couple of months maybe." The student said he did not know if any students were successful.

Clarence Kohbe, who teaches computer classes at the school, said he had heard student joke about breaking the system. "I took it to be a big joke," he said. "Some of the kids like to steal each others passwords and things like that, but I never thought they would try something like this."

Jose Jude, president of AES, said he doubted anyone really hacked into the system. "More than likely," he said, "they found a list of teachers passwords or something like that. The system is too sophisticated for a 14 year old to break." The company plans to send one of their experts to Lincoln High to help school officials deal with the problem.

Kohbe said he suspected that the students may have found a way to hack into the school's computers and to get teacher's passwords.

They likely changed other students' grades, not their own, because they are "very, very smart kid," Brown said. "These are not your average students. "They've been around computers for a long time, have computers at home, and go to hacker [Web] sites to learn how to do this."

School officials received an anonymous tip from a student about grade changing some months ago.

"Some of our teachers said they had also heard talk," Browne said. "So we took the tip seriously. We questioned the boy accused by the anonymous tip and checked his grades. We couldn't find anything, and his grades were alright."

The investigation was re-opened last week when a teacher noticed that a zero she had given a student had been changed to a 100. When that student was questioned, he broke down and cried. He admitted he had paid a student $5 to change the grade. The student said he had heard about the grade change racket several weeks before.

EXERCISE 73   NAME _____

Who is the top student in this year's graduating class at Lake Eenee High School?

Parents of a student have asked the Cicero County Court to decide. The problem centers around a college level wine class and a complicated formula for grades.

When class rankings came out in January, Joseph Javier topped the class and Suzannes Wimmer had the second-highest grade-point average, But Wimmer will be recognized at next week's graduation as valedictorian.

This does not sit well with Javier and his parents, who have filed suit against school district officials. Javier's attorney, Barbara Moody, has asked a judge to order the school to delay graduation ceremonies until the matter is settled.

"It's been frustrating," said Javier, who plans to attend Harvard. "Nobody at the school considers me No. 2. If I tell someone the story, they don't believe me."

Javier says, he simply followed the rules. A guidance councilor agreed that he could take "World of Wines," a geography class at Northern State University.

Lake Eenee, a highly competitive private high school, adopted a formula a few years ago to account for students who take college level classes. While an A in a regular high school course counts four points, an A in a college level class counts 6.

Javier took the wine class and two others at NSU and received As in each of them. Wimmer also took 3 NSU classes and received As.

However, Christy Wimmer, Suzannes's mother, complained to Principal Peter Voelz. She pointed out the school's handbook has numerous references forbidding students from using alcohol.

"How can you tell students on one hand not to drink and then give them college credit for learning how to drink" she asked, "How can you let a 17 year old enroll in a wine tasting class?"

Principal Voelz agreed. "We don't want there to be any implication that the administration of Lake Eenee supports or approves of under-aged drinking," he said. He decided that the school would not recognize the wine class.

That dropped Javier's grade point average from 5.33 to 5.137. Wimmers average is 5.142.

When Javier was looking for college-level courses, he listed on his proposed class schedule the wine class, described as a look at the "role of wine in modern culture" in an NSU course summary. Guidance councilor Bob Burdette approved the course which is taught in NSU's Sociology Department. "I should have read the course description more carefully," he told the schools Board of Governors at an emergency meeting Tuesday.

Javier said he did not participate in the wine tasting at the end of each class because he's not of legal drinking age. But, he says, he learned a lot about cultures of different parts of the world.

"Its the hardest class I've ever taken," he said. "It included sociology, history, the Roman expansion, agriculture, growing regions. I used what I learned in the class to write about Chilean wine on my [Advanced Placement] world history test."

Principal Voelz said the grade from the wine class will appear on Wimmers transcripts. He said state law requires all courses to be listed. But, he said, each school can decide what courses count toward a students gpa and how to choose the school valedictorian.

Voelz said he plans to recognize both students at the graduation ceremony but has not yet figured out exactly how.

EXERCISE 74   NAME _____

The former director of Northern State University's educational support department stole cash and took home thousands of dollars worth of electronic equipment, according to accusations in a university investigation report.

Belinda Marger, 49, resigned in April after Provost Marcella Jones recommended to the Regents she be fired after working 22 years for the university.

Details of the investigation was released Tuesday after a public records request by *The Blaster*, the NSU student newspaper.

The investigation into Marger's conduct was sparked by complaints from a employee in her department.

Marger could not be reached for comment Tuesday.

According to the university report, the unnamed employee told a university official that Marger went with him to Home Depot in July of last year and purchased about $1,000 worth of supplies, most of which was taken to Marger's home. Among those items taken to her home, he said, was three ceiling fans. He said he hung one in her kitchen and two on an outside patio.

"She told me, Don't you say anything to anyone, because if you do, I'm through with you," the employee is quoted as telling officials.

When confronted by university officials, the accusations were denied. Marger said the employee was lying in an attempt to get back at her for telling him he was lazy, the report said.

"He wasn't a happy camper about that," she said in the report.

On another occasion the employee said an overhead TV projection system had been sent to a local shop for repairs. When the repairs completed, Marger told him to pick up the system and take it to her son-in-laws house.

He said the device was listed on university records for months as being in the shop. "I know because we were getting lots of calls from pushy professors wanting to know when that thing would be back in the lecture hall," the employee was quoted as saying. It was not returned until the start of classes in the fall, he said.

Once investigators began questioning Marger about such practices, she returned a 27-inch TV and a number of other school items, including a lap-top computer, a digital camera, a scanner, a pager, a cell-phone, two Palm Pilots and a calculator, the report said.

Marger produced documents showing that she had signed out some of the items for temporary use. On the receipts were the initials of her secretary Mayra Hernandez. Hernandez later told district officials that Marger had her sign the receipts after the university started looking into Marger's activities, not before. Hernandez told her that she was 'trying out the equipment at home to make sure it worked OK'.

EXERCISE 75 NAME _____

For more than six decades, Mom's Country Cookin' was an institution in Elmwood.

Families gathered there after church. Teens from Lincoln High School gobbled down the trade-mark Blue Devil Sundays a marshmellow and ice cream concoction named after the schools football team. Business leaders depended on Mom's for a quick lunch.

And Mom's Bar next door to the restaurant was a sports bar long before the term 'sports bar' came into existence. Oldtimers say the bar was one of the first places in the county to have television and was the first place around with big screen TV and satellite.

Then in February, a 29-year-old woman died of liver failure after eating a meal of chicken wings and cheese fries from Mom's.

Health officials, already alarmed at what appeared to be a growing outbreak of hepatitis A in state, soon linked the woman's death to a Mom's cook, that had been diagnosed with the disease. Five other people, who survived the liver virus, were found to have eaten at the restaurant.

Reaction from customers was swift. Sickened by descriptions of how it is spread, the restaurant lost most of its regular customers.

Moms shut their doors two week's ago. Cooks and waitresses were shunned in their search for other jobs.

Owner Victor Montes, who's great grandmother opened Moms after her husband died, said he has been ruined financially.

"It's destroyed my life," said Montes, who disputes investigators certainty that the woman, Sloan Martin, contracted the disease from his cook or that his business had poor sanitation. "This is my families legacy. And now it's gone."

County health officials believe the incidence of hepatis is three times higher here than in the rest of the nation. They believe the county's large number of methamphetamine users are responsible for the disease. The disease is transmited by them through sex and by sharing drug paraphernalia. Lack of cleanliness can cause it to spread to their families and the general population.

Sloan is the only person in the county thought to have died from the virus. In February a 48 year old man needed a liver transplant after contracting the disease at a church fish fry, which also infected 15 others.

APPENDIX

ANSWERS TO PRACTICE EXERCISES

EXERCISE 6

STORY 1

NSU (**spell out unless local style says otherwise**) **Provost** Marcella Jones suspended on Tuesday a **history professor** who has been charged with soliciting for prostitution.

Police arrested **Professor** Carl J. Dow Sunday night at **Fifth** Street and Vine Avenue, an area known for prostitution, after he **allegedly** offered a **19-year-old** police cadet money in exchange for a sex act. City police were conducting an undercover operation along a **12-block** segment of Vine Avenue. **They arrested** 34 men and **three** women on a variety of solicitation and prostitution charges.

According to police records, Dow was convicted of a similar charge in Issaquah, **Wash.,** on **Dec. 5, 1993,** and was sentenced to **30** hours of community service.

At his arraignment Tuesday, Dow, 43, **367 E. 11th St.,** pleaded not guilty. His trial is set for **April 1.**

Dow's attorney, Laura Fulton, said Dow told her that he thought the woman was a student in one of his classes and had asked her if she wanted a ride only because she was walking in a bad neighborhood.

(**Omit Provost**) Jones said that Dow will be suspended with pay until the matter is settled. She said the **university** was never informed of his conviction in Washington.

(**Omit Prof.**) Dow has taught at the **university** for **10** years and is chair of its 3-year-old Roosevelt Center. He has written **two** books and 15 articles on the history of the **Navy.**

STORY 2

A British professor visiting Northern State University's campus died Tuesday shortly after a car hit him as he walked across **North Ninth Street** in front of the Science Building, police said.

Dr. John Wilkin, 68, of York, England, was struck about 2:30 **p.m.** He was pronounced dead on arrival at Northern City Hospital.

Two **NSU** professors walking behind (**omit Dr.**) **Wilkin** (**not Wilkins**) said he looked right instead of left to check for **oncoming** traffic. He then stepped off the curb in front of a car driven by Billy James Currant, 23, 234 **S. Eighth Ave.** Vehicles in the United Kingdom drive on the opposite side of the street.

Police said Currant, an NSU graduate student in psychology, was not charged. He was treated at Northern City Hospital for shock.

Wilkin, a physicist at the University of York, was in the **United States** visiting other scientists who are doing research in propulsion. He was to address a graduate **physics** class (**omit Tuesday night**) and to be the guest of honor at a reception Tuesday night.

EXERCISE 8

1. accept
2. effects, affected
3. passed, adverse
4. 5, aide
5. 19-year-old, nothing
6. alumnus, acting, Mayor
7. among
8. anticipated
9. arbitrator
10. arrested on a charge of
11. are
12. is
13. '02, A's
14. back up, backyard
15. bloc
16. break-in, four, buses

EXERCISE 9

Northern State University officials may have to turn down $900,000 left to the university because of the unusual demands the donor made, according to Northern State **President** Richard Aster.

To receive the money, **NSU** must rename ~~their~~ **its political science department** in honor of a man ~~arrested for allegedly~~ **once accused of or once charged with** trying to blow up an **Army (U.S. is not needed because it is obviously a U.S. Army base)** base in Florida during World War II.

The grant is part of a ~~$10,000,000~~ **$10 million** gift being offered to several universities by Dr. Homer Schmidt, a Charleston, ~~Illinois,~~ **Ill.,** internist who ran for **president** of the United States **four** times on a variety of antiwar tickets in the 1960s and '70s.

(Omit Dr.) Schmidt's will specified how the money is to be divided ~~between ten~~ **among 10** universities and gave detailed instructions for its use. If any university turns down the grant, ~~their~~ **its** money will be added to the gifts to the other universities.

An **aide** to ~~Governor~~ **Gov.** Alonzo Childres said the **governor** first learned of the will Tuesday. **(Omit Gov.)** Childres said he had asked **university** officials to consider the donor's background before ~~excepting~~ **accepting** the money. ~~Since~~ **Because** it is a private gift to NSU, the **governor** cannot order the university to refuse it.

(Omit Pres.) ~~Astor~~ **Aster (spell as on first reference)** said NSU officials also feared ~~averse~~ **adverse** reactions from the public. "I'm afraid changing the name of the department might ~~effect~~ **affect** the image of Northern State University in the community," he said. "We can't be sure what effect something like this might have." He said he had appointed a ~~three-man~~ **three-person or appointed three people to a (to avoid sexism)** committee to review the proposal and had asked Vice **(no hyphen)** President Martha Boone to chair it.

The NSU Faculty Senate **(AP would lowercase Faculty Senate, but many papers would use caps)** Tuesday ~~passed~~ **adopted or approved** a resolution opposing the measure. ~~They~~ **It** had already ~~passed~~ **adopted or approved** an amendment to ~~their~~ **its** bylaws requiring ~~their~~ **its** approval of name changes on campus.

Etta Cunning, **president** of the Faculty Senate **(see above)**, said sentiment on campus is against the gift. "You just can't name departments after **anyone** that **(who if your paper corrects grammar in quotes)** gives the school a bunch of money," she said.

(Omit Prof.) Cunning said she knew Schmidt and ~~anticipated~~ **expected** that he might leave money to the school. However, she said she had no idea what restrictions he would place on the money and had made no plans for how to handle the gift.

(Omit Dr.) Schmidt's will requires NSU to name its political science department after Clarence Wilson, an **alumnus** of the university. Wilson was ~~arrested for alleged~~ **charged with** treason and attempted murder in 1942 after a bomb **(omit allegedly unless there is a debate over whether a bomb exploded)** exploded near **an Army** troop train in Panacea, **Fla.** The charges were later dropped.

The will also established a scholarship fund at NSU and specified the first **four** recipients. They were Mark White, 19, 1459 **S. Park Ave.**; Mary Williams, 20, 120 N. Fifth St.; Clyde Overdorf, 32, 2315 **W. Johnson Drive**; and Sidney Jones, 22, 234 **E. 12th Ave.** The will says that future scholarship must be given "to brave students who fight the system."

EXERCISE 11

1. mayor, streets
2. Capitol
3. parties, cave in
4. Charleston, capital
5. Churchgoers, clean up
6. co-author, cooperate, coordinate
7. its, their
8. its
9. compliment, complimentary
10. Congress
11. Constitution, constitutional
12. to
13. with
14. of, in Celina, (comma) Tenn., (comma) and Glascow, (comma), Ky., (comma)
15. convince, copyright
16. persuade
17. cover-up, cutbacks, cut off

EXERCISE 13

PART 1

1. die-hard, 7-footer
2. East (assuming it refers to the Eastern United States), 2 feet, north (the direction)
3. discreet
4. dived, $10,000
5. door to door, rundown
6. countdown, drunken
7. was
8. emigrated
9. engine (if the reporter was referring to large jet engines that propel the plane)
10. ensure, envelope
11. Every day, extramarital, Everyone
12. fazed, federal
13. fewer
14. less (some amount of money between zero and $20, not necessarily whole dollars. She may have had $14.53—which is not countable dollar bills.)
15. firefighter, flare
16. first-degree
17. first quarter, flair
18. follow-up, french, Swiss
19. front-page, part time, front line
20. fund-raising, full-time

PART 2

1. Waiting for the ambulance to arrive, he felt the pain grow intense and thought he would die. **OR** As he waited for the ambulance to arrive, the pain grew intense and he thought he would die.
2. Missing for three days, the girl's body was found lying in a pool of blood.
3. Correct as written.
4. After Johnson received more than $1 million in campaign contributions, reporters believed he was unbeatable.

PART 3

1. Darryl Johnson, who won Saturday's race, was later disqualified.
2. Officials said he had used a gasoline additive that had been outlawed.
3. Bill's Meat Market, which sold the spoiled meat, has been sued by three parents whose children suffered food poisoning.

EXERCISE 15

1. ninth-graders, 10th graders.
2. was, grisly
3. halfhearted, half-baked
4. hung, handmade
5. hometown, hold up
6. suffered, cave-in
7. It's, its
8. its, federal, government
9. lie
10. laid
11. lying
12. Sen., Rep.
13. long-distance

EXERCISE 17

1. are
2. marshal, mantel
3. middle class, middle-class
4. Gen., mph
5. general, $3 million
6. accident
7. mix up, Lions'
8. Lions, is
9. multimillionaire, Mount
10. is, agree
11. 3-2, two, 10, protesters
12. 10th Avenue and Second Street.
13. send-off, stop off, playoffs
14. flameout, outdated
15. stopover, take over
16. the firefighter fought back tears

EXERCISE 19

SECTION 1

1. Page 4, Page 1
2. Sen., R-Minn., part-time
3. part time, Party).
4. 4, percent, was, 70, percent, were
5. period
6. persuaded
7. convinced
8. pleaded
9. churches, playoffs
10. principal, principal, principles
11. Professor, jail
12. profile, pro-labor
13. Passers-by, attorneys general
14. ravaged
15. right-wingers, party
16. second-guess, secondhand
17. second-rate, semitropical
18. spokesman

SECTION 2.

1. Bill **Jones'** daughter won an award in Judy **Schultz's** speech class.
2. **Tuesday's** paper said the Legislature plans to cut the Northern State University budget.
3. The **attorneys** general of Maine and Iowa filed reports with the **president's** legal staff.
4. Five police officers saw the incident. The **officers'** statements differed. One **officer's** report said he found cocaine hidden in the **man's** pants. Two of the **officers'** reports said they found cocaine in the **women's** purses.
5. The **Joneses** came to the concert, but the Whites decided to go to the party. Their **children's** babysitter had to be home by 11 **p.m.**
6. Five **cities** plan to sue the county over its plans to reduce patrols by deputies within the cities. **It's** the first time a city has sued the county.
7. The professor said that **Marx's** philosophy is much like **Jesus'** philosophy.
8. The event is for **7- and 8-year-olds.**

SECTION 3.

referred	controlled	totaled	quarreled	backward	offered
canceled	referring	totaling	sizable	quizzed	modeled
abused	combating	omitted	recurring	hauled	occurred
allotted	conferred	recurred	alleged	toward	
bused to school					

EXERCISE 21

1. take over, takeoff
2. teachers college
3. Tonight's, televised, 9, nothing
4. minus, 5, higher
5. that, nothing
6. president's, 9 p.m.
7. Sen., Professor, oil baron
8. holdup, walk-up
9. clean up, grown-up,
10. T-shirt, U-turn
11. vice president, United States, Senate
12. 4-pound, 6 pounds
13. who
14. who
15. whoever
16. whomever
17. yearlong, wrongdoing, year-end, past

EXERCISE 23

1. Consolidated Computer Co. **N** on Tuesday **N** began to buy back computers **N** with defective chips **N**.
2. Customers **N** who **P** purchased computers **N** with SV16 chips **N** have four months **N** to claim their **P** refunds **N**.
3. After Jackson **N** was fired, he **P** hacked his **P** way **N** into the computers **N** and stole the secret formulas **N**.
4. is
5. it, was
6. was
7. were
8. were
9. was
10. were
11. were, is
12. it, its
13. has, its
14. have
15. has
16. its
17. was
18. they reach
19. it
20. his
21. has
22. their, their
23. were
24. has
25. recommend
26. emphasizes, their
27. was
28. were
29. were
30. say
31. favors
32. ask, four-door
33. reduces
34. full-size, are
35. Chicago-based, believes
36. A team of officials from the Federal Aviation Administration and the Boeing Corporation ~~are~~ **is** studying the airplane's flight recorders.
37. Shortly before the crash, the crew told air controllers that **it was** having trouble controlling the plane. **Or: Crew members** told air controllers that **they were** having trouble controlling the plane.
38. Boeing pledged that it will fix any problems found in **its** airplanes.
39. On the team **are** Jorge Santana and Thurmond Maxwell.
40. After two rounds, the **first-place** team **is** Betsy Tuggle and Paul Masson (**comma**) but Joyce Lacy and Roy Copeland are still the best team in the tourney.
41. Memphis will begin **its** season against a Knoxville team that already **has** won two games.

EXERCISE 25

1. For **PREP** the first **ADJ** time **OP** in **PREP** 50 **ADJ** years **OP**, angry **ADJ** customers can seek help from **PREP** a government **ADJ** agency **OP**
2. The law received overwhelming **ADJ** support from **PREP** consumer **ADJ** groups **OP**.
3. The House passed the bill unanimously **ADV**, but in **PREP** the Senate **OP** it was debated bitterly **ADV**.
4. The newly **ADV** appointed **ADJ** attorney was angry **ADJ** when the judge quickly **ADV** denied her request for **PREP** a postponement **OP**.
5. The aging **ADJ** factories on **PREP** the Ohio River **OP** belched sooty **ADJ** smoke.
6. Stores **no comma** on Main Street **no comma** are quickly becoming profitable.
7. Neither the mayor nor the City Council ~~have~~ **has** helped build trust.
8. The City Council should reconsider ~~their~~ **its** plans for the area.
9. The merchants and the Chamber of Commerce ~~is~~ **are** planning a celebration.
10. Either the officers or the mayor is lying.
11. The fire **no comma** at the Bosford Box Company **no comma** burned for hours.
12. Neither the incumbent nor his challengers were willing to debate.
13. Police seized the newly painted car.

EXERCISE 27

1. The council S approved AV funding for road improvements but rejected AV plans for a bike path.
2. Most S of the improvements will be LV to roads around Quality Fair Shopping Mall.
3. The new roads S will allow AV easy access to the mall from Route 50.
4. Without the road improvements, the planning board S would not approve AV the expansion.
5. The mall S is LV the largest shopping facility in the county.
6. Mayor Roberta Simms S campaigned AV against the expansion but then voted AV for it.
7. Simms S was widely criticized PV by voters who S thought AV she S had betrayed AV them.
8. Honesty S in government was LV a theme in her campaign.
9. Traffic S around the mall has grown AV dramatically in the past 10 years.
10. The expansion S will make AV a bad situation even worse, according to many residents.
11. The decision S was based PV on a 3-year-old report, the residents S said AV.
12. Four new lanes S will be added PV to Georgia Street between Kings Avenue and 39th Street.
13. Fifteen years ago the area S was LV a peaceful valley with few homes and quaint shops.
14. Mall owners' plans S include AV a new department store, specialty shops and a food court.
15. Many shoppers S hope AV that the new stores S will offer AV more selection and that the added competition S will bring AV prices down.
16. Two hunters discovered dinosaur bones on the banks of White River.
17. [Whichever agency filed the charges] charged Northern State University President Richard Aster on Tuesday with first-degree murder in the death of the president of the NSU faculty senate.
18. Waves battered Mississippi beaches for a second straight day Tuesday as Hurricane Lola continued to stir up the Gulf of Mexico. [Check story context to make sure waves were doing the battering. It may not be correct to say that Lola was battering the beaches.]
19. The City Council passed a law prohibiting overnight parking of large trucks and recreational vehicles on city streets.
20. Organizers canceled Tuesday's concert after they received a bomb threat. [Check story context to make sure the organizer—and not public safety people—canceled the concert.]
21. lay
22. lie
23. lie
24. lay
25. lay
26. lay
27. laid

EXERCISE 29

1. Before McCoy discovered the joys of journalism (**comma**) she was a chemistry major.
2. Although the Yankees won the pennant (**comma**) the team's owner fired the manager and criticized the team's dedication.
3. Angry fans threw coins at the referees (**comma**) and officials cleared the arena and gave the victory to the Wildcats.
4. The prosecutor pointed his finger and called the youths "murderous misfits."
5. After pointing his finger at the youths (**comma**) the prosecutor called them "murderous misfits."
6. After the prosecutor pointed his finger at the youths (**comma**) he called them "murderous misfits."
7. The Cubs will play the Braves on Tuesday at Wrigley Field (**comma**) but the White Sox have the day off to recover after losing Monday's doubleheader.
8. Bob Smith was convicted of bank robbery but found not guilty of the murder of the guard (**comma**) according to court records.
9. Police said the governor was not present when the crime occurred.
10. General Motors increased the prices on its cars (**comma**) but Ford and Chrysler announced price cuts.
11. An AP reporter was told about the senator's decision and quickly filed her story.
12. An AP reporter was told about the senator's decision (**comma**) but her editors decided the story was too speculative and refused to use it.
13. Reporters lose their tempers when editors make such decisions.
14. The reporter threatened to sue the editors (**semicolon**) however (**comma**) no one thought she was serious. *Or:* The reporter threatened to sue the editors. However, no one thought she was serious.
15. The boy was found (**no comma**) in Dallas (**no comma**) with four other runaways.
16. Running a major corporation (**comma**) Tidler had little time for his family.
17. Running a major corporation (**no comma**) often strains relationships.
18. The company (**S**) will buy (**V**) traffic lights for the intersection (**comma**) and the city (**S**) will pay (**V**) to widen the road.
19. After having (**P**) breakfast with Baptist ministers, the governor (**S**) spoke (**V**) to supporters at a Unitarian church.
20. Suffering (**P**) from a severe case of tennis elbow, Myers (**S**) withdrew from a tournament in Rome (**comma**) but she (**S**) said (**V**) she (**S**) will play (**V**) in the French Open next month

EXERCISE 31

1. The president of Consolidated Airlines said the company was losing money.
2. After Consolidated Airline's stock dropped more than 40 points in a single day (**comma**) many investors decided to sell all their stock in transportation companies.
3. Seeing Consolidated Airline's stock drop more than 40 points in a single day caused many investors to sell all their holdings in transportation companies.
4. Giving smokeless tobacco to children under 16 will be against the law if the bill passes.
5. Flying through a thunderstorm (**comma**) the plane was struck by lightning.
6. The plane was not damaged even though it was struck by lightning.
7. After Tompkins finished writing a biography of Truman (**comma**) she began a mystery novel.
8. Tompkins finished writing a biography of Truman and then began work on a novel.
9. Tompkins had just finished writing a biography of Truman when she began work on a novel.
10. After speaking with his client (**comma**) the lawyer accepted the plea bargain.
11. He told the prosecutor that his client had information about the mob.
12. He said (**comma**) **"My** client can spill the beans on more bad guys than you know about."
13. Although union leaders say they want an early settlement (**comma**) they will not accept pay cuts of any kind.
14. One union leader said company officials were "fat cats of the worse kind."
15. After dropping the fly in the fifth inning (**comma**) Smith hammered a home run in the eighth.

EXERCISE 33

1. Fifteen students who were arrested at Saturday's game were expelled today by Provost Marcella Jones (**comma**) who said she was ashamed of the students' conduct.
2. Professor Claude Wilkens (**comma**) who admitted he took bribes from students (**comma**) was fired.
3. People who hope to make a living writing must be versatile.
4. Families ~~that~~ **who** lost children in Tuesday's crash have sued the Acme Bus Company (**comma**) which leased the bus to the church.
5. Northern Brewery Inc. is expected to buy Southern Beer (**comma**) ~~who~~ **which** recently fired ~~their~~ **its** CEO.
6. Professors who will get pay raises under the new agreement praised union leaders. Whether to use commas depends on meaning of sentences. If you place commas, the sentence means that all professors will get pay raises and all of them are praising union leaders. If the sentence does not have the commas, it means that only some professors will get raises and they are the ones who are praising union leaders.
7. Tompkins (**comma**) who finished writing a biography of Truman last week (**comma**) is now working on a novel.
8. Married students who live on campus pay more for housing than single students do.
9. Bette Xavier (**comma**) who lives in Clarke Hall (**comma**) said she may sue the university unless ~~they change~~ **it changes** the policy.
10. Police said the woman ~~that~~ **who** robbed the ~~7-11~~ **7-Eleven** on Main Street used a toy pistol.
11. Police said they have no information about who robbed the bank.
12. The World Cup (**comma**) **which** ~~that~~ is played every four years (**comma**) showcases the world's best soccer players.
13. Students who saw the incident disagreed with Sheriff Bill Bianchi (**comma**) who said the shooting was justified.
14. Maurice Daniels (**comma**) who won the lottery (**comma**) said he will quit his ~~part-time~~ **part-time** job.
15. Microsoft (**comma**) **which** ~~that~~ makes the Windows operating system (**comma**) said ~~they~~ **it** will sue any company ~~who~~ **that** violates ~~their~~ **its** copyrights.
16. A journalism professor who promised his classes he would not assign homework was named teacher of the year by the student body.

EXERCISE 35

1. The mismanaged bookstore allegedly had not paid federal taxes for the past five years.
2. The ~~well-dressed~~ well-dressed attorney walked quickly from the meeting and said he would never return.
3. Unruly fans angrily booed the referees and frequently threw cups of beer onto the basketball court.
4. Neither the workers nor the company is willing to discuss the yearlong strike.
5. A steady downpour drenched the ~~bone-dry~~ bone-dry city and tied up ~~rush-hour~~ rush-hour traffic.
6. Police said the ~~hold-up~~ holdup man ordered the bank guard to lay down his weapon.
7. The ~~out-of-work~~ out-of-work man said he needed a ~~part-time~~ part-time job to buy Christmas presents.
8. His wife works full time at a motel that pays notoriously low wages.
9. The burly, ~~310-pound~~ 310-pound lineman called the report a "setup job by ~~good-for-nothing~~ good-for-nothing reporters."
10. The senator proposed a bill that would allow **18-year-olds** to drink beer.
11. The coroner said the **3-month-old** baby had a **6-inch** slash across her back.
12. The **Cincinnati-based** company paid **12-year-old boys** to sell the **second-rate** candy door to door.
13. The gangsters planned to walk out of prison and head for their **hide-out**. (The AP spelling is in the *–out* section of the stylebook.)
14. The doctor apologized to the worried man and said there was a **mix-up** in the records.
15. The doctor said the man's **checkup** did not indicate that he was headed for a mental **breakdown** after all.
16. The **overrated** medic said the **X-rays** were **upside-down** when he very hurriedly glanced at them.
17. The doctor said he was completely embarrassed by the first mistake he had made in his long (**comma**) distinguished career. "I've behaved like a silly (**comma**) incompetent intern," he said.
18. The patient (**comma**) who was much too angry to talk (**comma**) reached into the pocket of his blue (**comma**) **double-breasted** suit and pulled out a business card.
19. He tried to steady his violently shaking hand before handing the brightly colored card to the doctor.
20. The card identified the patient as a **personal-injury** attorney who specialized in medical malpractice.

EXERCISE 40

1. charged with
2. sentenced to, prison
3. convicted of
4. suffered
5. crashed into, concrete
6. alumna
7. Since
8. Because
9. affect
10. centered on
11. fiscal
12. persuaded
13. persuade
14. convinced
15. a while, from speaking
16. backward, aid
17. than
18. under way
19. ensure
20. Parents who earn more than $40,000 and own their own homes cannot receive tuition rebates.
21. All Jackson wanted out of life was to play in the NFL and to drive a red Porsche sports car. *Or* All Jackson wanted out of life was an NFL career and a red Porsche sports car.
22. People who frequently go on fad diets suffer muscle loss. *Or* Frequently people who go on fad diets suffer muscle loss.
23. Despite the number of complaints, the company promised to recall only 100 cars.
24. The coach promised the alumni association his team would fill the stadium and win a conference championship. *Or* The coach promised the alumni association sellouts for every home game and a conference championship.
25. After praying for peace, the pope visited the hospital and talked to many wounded soldiers.
26. Based in Texas, the company is the nation's largest producer of salsa.
27. The new school superintendent promised to ensure that every high school student received extensive training in computer science. [See if the New Mexico angle can be worked in more naturally elsewhere in the story.] *Or* The new school superintendent promised that every high school student will receive extensive training in computer science.

EXERCISE 42

1. Trying to keep pace with its rapid growth (**comma**) Northern State University on Tuesday announced plans for four new residence halls.
2. Having loved the book (**comma**) fans of Clancy's novels were disappointed by the movie. *Or* Although fans of Clancy's novels loved the book, they were disappointed by the movie.
3. After graduating from college (**comma**) she made finding a job her next goal. *Or* After he graduated from college, his next goal was a job.
4. After slugging the police officer (**comma**) the woman escaped on a mountain bike.
5. Having been out of school for five years, she was surprised by the attitudes of many of the students.
6. After lowering its admission standards (**comma**) Buckley accepted more students this year.
7. Knowing the source of his problems (**comma**) he vowed never to drink again.
8. Having been identified by three witnesses (**comma**) Murphy was charged with the crime. *Or* After Murphy was identified by three witnesses, police charged her with the crime.
9. After Wilson agreed to testify against his friend, charges against him were dropped.
10. Blessed with warm (**comma**) sunny weather (**comma**) Spain is popular with tourists. *Or* Because Spain is blessed with warm, sunny weather, tourists flock there.
11. Having two prior felony convictions (**comma**) Jefferson feared he would receive a life sentence.
12. Seeing the storm approaching (**comma**) referees ordered the players to leave the field.
13. Having arrived an hour late, the attorney was fined $100 for contempt of court. *Or* Because the attorney arrived an hour late, the judge fined him $100 for contempt of court.
14. After Thompson walked the first three batters, the crowd cheered when he finally threw a strike. *Or* After walking the first three batters, Thompson was cheered by the crowd when he finally threw a strike.
15. Having worked on the copy desk of my college newspaper, I would like a career as a copy editor.
16. Having a strong command of grammar, Stewart finds copy editing to be easy. *Or* Because Stewart has a strong command of grammar, copy editing is easy for her.
17. After losing a costly suit to the worker's widow, [the department or company] focused more attention on employee safety. *Or* After the company lost a costly suit to the worker's widow, more attention was focused on employee safety.
18. Hoping to increase attendance at home games, [the team or the university] lowered ticket prices. *Or* [The team or the university] lowered ticket prices in hopes of increasing attendance at home games. *Or* Ticket prices were lowered in hopes of increasing attendance at home games.

EXERCISE 45

1. The coach said he will not start Williamson in the home opener.
2. Williamson said, (**comma**) "**My** arm feels great. I'm ready to go."
3. The trainer, however, said, "I don't think he's ready. (**no quote marks**) We don't want to lose him for the season." (If these two sentences were not said together, the reporter should rewrite the passage so as not to give that impression.)
4. According to university records (**comma**) O'Hara never attended the school.
5. "Why did you lie about where you went to **college?**" the prosecutor asked O'Hara.
6. "You had to have a degree to get a job with Consolidated **Airlines**," **O'Hara answered. "I** knew I could fly the planes. So I just told them I had a degree. I didn't think it would matter in the long run." *Or* O'Hara answered, "**You** had to have a degree to get a job with Consolidated Airlines. I knew I could fly the planes. So I just told them I had a degree. I didn't think it would matter in the long run."
7. The prime minister said the agreement could lead to "**peace** in our **time.**"
8. The mayor said she decided to run again "after months of soul-searching and talks with my family."
9. "Why would anyone want to ride a bike without **a helmet?**" **the doctor asked. "We** have people in the emergency room every week with severe head injuries that could have been **prevented.**" *Or* **The doctor said, "Why** would anyone want to ride a bike without a **helmet? We** have people in the emergency room every week with severe head injuries that could have been **prevented.**"
10. "Either the **Legislature** gives us more money or we cut programs," NSU **President** Richard Aster responded. "We can not continue as we are. We have raised student fees as high as the law **allows,** and we've slashed the budget every way imaginable. I can't tell you all the ways that those cuts have **affected** the quality of our programs. (**no quote marks**)

    "The legislators must find more money for higher education, especially for NSU. If they **don't,** (**comma**) we'll begin dropping whole areas of study."

    Or

    "Either the **Legislature** gives us more money or we cut programs," NSU **President** Richard Aster responded. "We can not continue as we are. We have raised student fees as high as the law allows, (**comma**) and we've slashed the budget every way imaginable. I can't tell you all the ways that those cuts have **affected** the quality of our programs.**" (quote marks)**

    "The legislators must find more money for higher education, especially for NSU,**" he said. "If** they **don't,** (**comma**) we'll begin dropping whole areas of study."

EXERCISE 48

Good editors could edit these stories differently. Compare yours to these.

STORY 1

Journalism students at Northern State University won't be using new computers for several months. The journalism department on Monday rejected the only bid it received for the new equipment because it was too high.

Professor Susan Pritchard said the department had hoped to replace the 20 aging computers in its graphics labs. She said the department will have to re-advertise for bids.

STORY 2

Rodney Darwin, president of Citizens Bank, will address the 10th annual awards banquet for the Northern State University Economics Club Saturday in place of Rep. William E. Greshaw, who will be in Washington for a special session of Congress.

EXERCISE 51

ASSIGNMENT 1

Story 1. Is "raided" an appropriate word? Or were police just called to the scene? Was there any significance to the party (a special occasion, for example)? How often do police receive complaints of loud parties at the fraternity?

What charges were filed against the students? Were they taken into custody? Have they bailed out? Any significance to the fact that one of those arrested was a 45-year-old woman (the mother of one of the men, employee of the fraternity, an entertainer)?

In another story soon, we might want to look into relations between fraternity houses and their neighbors.

Story 2. What kinds of criticisms were contained in the letter the student wrote? Any quotes from student and faculty leaders—or students and faculty on campus—about how they reacted to the apology? Have there been any other incidents in which the president showed he had a quick temper or vindictive streak?

Can we talk to the student and see how he's reacting to all this?

Story 3. A quarter of a million dollars is a lot of money for a bed! What makes this bed so valuable?

The second graph says they "cut their way" through a back door. The detective says they used "a sophisticated way" to get through the door. Are those statements consistent? Will the detective be more specific about the "sophistication" idea?

Do police have any theories about the theft? How easy is it to fence a $250,000 bed?

ASSIGNMENT 2

Line 8. Capitalize university.
Line 9. standing-room-only crowd; AP lower-cases student senate. Check local style.
Line 12. Aster said. "I
Line 15. Capitalize Legislature.
Line 16. Resolutions are adopted or approved. (Also, it would be *passed*, not *past*.)
Line 17. high-ranking
Line 23. Main and Jackson streets.
Line 24. Police said burglars
Line 25. shop, not shoppe.
Line 29. five minutes.
Line 30. at the shop Saturday.

EXERCISE 55

ASSIGNMENT 1

The lead is based on the comments of the center's director who says the center has been well-received. It is pretty much what one might expect she'd say and may sound self-serving. There may be a stronger lead—one that might attract readers—in the fact that mothers enroll their unborn babies in the program. An editor might suggest that the reporter see if that angle could be played in the lead.

ASSIGNMENT 2

The story is based mostly on a single source, the director of the center. Might there be other sources who might be able to give the story a broader perspective? The dean of the school of education perhaps or student government leaders? And might there be a follow-up story in the size issue? What about all those students whose children can't get into the center? What does the university do for them?

ASSIGNMENT 3

Line 1. well-received
Line 4. 3- to 5-year-olds
Line 6. day-care, delete Dr.
Line 10. full-time, the quote probably needs attribution (Myers said).
Line 16. Delete Dr., pregnant women.
Lines 17 and 18. names like 'Angel Williams' or 'Baby Smith.'" *Or* you could omit the quotes around the names.
Line 25. Delete Dr.; Myers, not Meyers; 3-year-olds
Line 29. The quote probably needs attribution (too large now," Myers said).
Line 30. New paragraph.
Line 32. day-care

EXERCISE 60

ASSIGNMENT 1

The story is very wordy so there are many ways to cut 30 words. Among the cuts you might have made:

Line 1. Drop "morning." Early Wednesday suggests morning.

Lines 1 and 2. "He was driving" isn't needed since police are unlikely to ticket someone who was not involved, and "at a crossing" is not needed because (1) that's where train-car accidents usually happen and (2) it's redundant since the idea is repeated in Line 5. Drop "Elwood" in "Elwood woman" to unclutter the lead.

Lines 3 and 4. Drop Elwood and same. Turn the passive clause "that engineers have been ticketed by Elwood police at the same crossing" into an active clause "that police have ticketed engineers at the crossing." Using active voice saves four words.

Lines 5 and 6. "Lucille McKinney, 42, Elwood, was crossing the tracks on State Road 28 near Main Street when her car was struck by a slow-moving Central Line engine." The description about the double tracks probably isn't needed. Add Elwood since it was deleted in the lead. Keep "slow-moving" so the reader could better understand the crash.

Lines 7, 8 and 9. The engine's headlights were off, the railroad gates and warning lights didn't work, and no flagman was present, police said.

Lines 10 and 11. "A violation of traffic laws" isn't needed.

Lines 12 and 13. "McKinney was treated at University Hospital in Elwood for minor cuts and a broken leg." Accident victims are usually taken by ambulance. The verb "treated" suggests that she was "treated and released."

Line 16. "He was driving" isn't needed.

ASSIGNMENT 2

Here's one version with 79 words.

ELWOOD—Police early Wednesday arrested the engineer of a train that collided with a car in downtown Elwood.

Lawrence Dillenger, 53, Oakwood, was cited for failing to use safety measures. Police said the Central Line engine wasn't lighted, the railroad gates and warning lights weren't working, and no flagman was present.

The car's driver, Lucille McKinney, 42, Elwood, suffered a broken leg and cuts.

Recently, police have charged two other engineers with traffic violations at the crossing.

EXERCISE 63

1. Mean = $4,300, Media = $3,000, Mode = $1,000
2. 15 percent
3. $26,250
4. a. 50 percent, b. 1 percentage point
5. Your county, 52 per 1,000; Neighboring county, 38 per 1,000.
6. 33 percent
7. 25 percent
8. The story might indicate that the race between Jimenez and Morganstern is within the margin of error and may be too close to call.
9. The copy editor might caution the reporter that the changes are within the margin of error. The apparent change may be caused as much by sampling error as by the endorsement.
10. Margin of error doesn't refer to any avoidable mistakes on the part of the pollsters. Margin of error refers to the statistical likelihood that the sample represents the total population (meaning that the sample has roughly the same percentage of Democrats, Republicans, drunkards, basketball fans, seniors, singles, marrieds, etc. as is in the population of the community.)

EXERCISE 66

Line 1. Martin Luther King is admired by people of all races. African-Americans will not be the only people who will pay their respects to him.

Line 2. A factual problem. His organization was the Southern Christian Leadership Council, not the NAACP.

Line 4. interfaith.

Line 6. The AP prefers to use "the Rev." with Roman Catholic priests.

Line 8. Check "Moslem church." It probably should be mosque.

Line 8. Check the correct name of Viceroy's affiliation. He may be with the Nation of Islam. Many members of that religion consider the term "Black Muslims" derogatory.

Line 10. King was assassinated in 1968, not 1986.

NOTES

NOTES

NOTES

NOTES

NOTES

NOTES

NOTES

Printed in the USA
CPSIA information can be obtained
at www.ICGtesting.com
JSHW060917271223
54120JS00016B/163